The Digital Marketing Handbook

To Mum and Dad. Thanks for always being my biggest cheerleaders and demonstrating what it means to lead with kindness and values.

AB x

PS: thanks for letting me quit school to try out this whole business thing... what a relief it's working out okay.

LAURENCE KING

First published in Great Britain in 2024 by Laurence King
An imprint of Quercus Editions Ltd
Carmelite House
50 Victoria Embankment
London EC4Y 0DZ

An Hachette UK company

A CIP catalogue record for this book is available from the British Library

TPB ISBN 978-1-52943-147-6
Ebook ISBN 978-1-52943-148-3

10 9 8 7 6 5 4 3 2 1

Designer: Charlotte Bolton
Commissioning editor: Liz Faber
Project editor: Catherine Hooper

Printed and bound in China by 1010 Printing International Ltd

Papers used by Quercus are from well-managed forests and other responsible sources.

The Digital Marketing Handbook

Create a Simple Strategy and Grow Your Business Online

Alice Benham

Contents

Introduction

Welcome to your new marketing handbook, a space for you to get the education, support and inspiration you need to grow online. I am VERY excited you're reading this, not only because I love seeing businesses grow, but also because I absolutely love marketing. And I have done since the day I stepped into the world of business.

I first came across marketing when I was seventeen years old, fresh out of school and beginning my very first freelance role. Despite having no experience, I was hired by a charity to manage their social media (probably because I was young and young people like social media... right?) and was thrown in at the deep end. I was Googling what terms like 'SEO' meant under the table at meetings and constantly realizing I was the youngest in the room, but I was undeterred as I was driven by my growing obsession.

Some may have seen my work as just writing tweets or scheduling blogs, but I could sense the vehicle for change that I had at my fingertips. I had the power to tell stories, build real community, change lives and, ultimately, reach a business's goals. It was a rollercoaster of learning underpinned by a growing curiosity for the new marketing world I was in.

Since then, that learning and obsession has only continued.

When I began building my own community and connecting with more businesses, I saw how overcomplicated marketing often felt to them. They were overwhelmed, scared, lacking time, unsure where to begin and struggling to achieve the results they desired and deserved.

I totally got it. You started a business because you love your thing – the product you create; the service you provide; the mission you're on. You didn't start out to become a copywriter, social media manager and marketing strategist all wrapped up into one, but that's the reality of growing a business in this modern age.

The growth of your business is significantly tied to your ability to market it. And this book is here to help you do just that. Here's what to expect:

- Proven and practical expertise
- Clear definitions (no jargon!)
- Quick tips
- Examples and case studies
- Insights from trusted experts
- Chapter summaries for easy reminders
- Action steps for every topic

No icky or fluffy tips in here, I promise!

You're going to read the word 'action' a LOT throughout this book, but I'm not sorry about it. Because in helping more than 10,000 students and clients with their marketing, action is the only secret to success I've ever come across. So my intention isn't for you to read this book, it's for you to use it.

Whether you're reading this book front to back for the full impact or picking out the chapters to spot-check your marketing, I hope you approach it with an open and action-oriented mindset.

I truly believe you are capable of being a great marketer.

Ready for me to show you how?

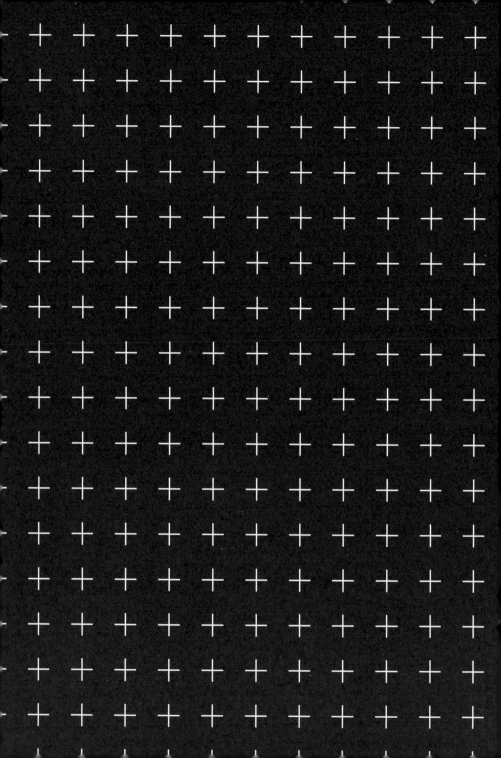

PART I

Get clarity

Clarity

When we approach our strategy with a clear foundation of clarity we have increased confidence, can narrow our focus and feel certain that what we're doing is the right fit for us.

Let's nail the why, what, who and how of our marketing strategy.

1.
Why marketing?

Marketing is a word that gets thrown around so much that I often wonder if it's lost its meaning. I'm a big believer in the power of bringing things back to basics so, before we proceed, let's clarify what marketing actually is.

Alice Benham Dictionary
Marketing: Using the voice of your business to reach new people, connect them to your work and nurture a community through the buyers' journey and towards the point of action.

To give some sub-definitions:

Voice of your business = any content or touch-points.
New people = your ideal client or customer or whoever is relevant to your mission.
Nurture a community = build their relationship with you and your offerings.
Towards the point of action = buy, book, email (whatever your end goal is).

When we strip away all the fluff and the fancy words, marketing is simply a conversation. A chat. The opportunity to connect.

Too often, I think we dehumanize marketing. We focus on analytics, and the fact that it's often accessed through a screen can suck the life out of it. But that's detrimental to marketing success. The more human we make it, the more we'll create conversations that actually connect with people and the better it will feel on both sides.

Why utilize marketing?

I'm confident that whoever you are, wherever you're at, you and/or your business could benefit from marketing in some way.

I could write this whole book about the benefits of intentional marketing, but to keep it brief, here are my top selling points for marketing:

1. Make more money by selling more.
2. Encourage repeat sales and generate a community that does the work for you.
3. Stand out from competitors.
4. Generate exposure with those who matter.
5. Get external opportunities – press, speaking, book deal (hint, hint...).
6. Build a network and connect with great people.

Throughout this book, you'll see case studies with real-life examples of businesses and lives that have been transformed through the correct utilization of marketing. So trust me when I say that this list is just the tip of the iceberg.

Now to make it more specific: why do *you* want to use marketing? 'Because I want to grow!'

Yeah, that answer isn't quite what I'm looking for, I'm afraid. I want you to get specific on your marketing goals.

Why? Because <u>action needs direction</u>.

One of the biggest reasons I see people struggling to show up and succeed with their marketing is because they have no direction. Marketing is full of opportunities and possibilities – almost too full. So full that without clear direction you'll struggle to navigate any of the following chapters. Marketing goals will help you to:

- Know which strategy is right for you.
- Ignore shiny-object syndrome and minimize comparisons.
- Measure results more effectively.
- Feel more motivated to show up.

Put simply, we need to know *why* before we look at what, how and where.

Having clear goals won't only help you know *what* to do, but will also stop you from being overwhelmed or distracted by *what not* to do – which can happen easily with marketing when there are so many options out there.

Business strategist and founder of the Owusu Collective Josephine Owusu says: 'Each piece of action you take should work towards your goals – anything that doesn't align with this is a distraction and should be put on hold.'

The purpose of a marketing goal is to outline what we want our marketing to achieve, specific to our business or situation. A great goal outlines both result and action, so let me walk you through how to do this effectively:

1. Result: Clarify your business vision and wider goals. Marketing is a tool to help you achieve your definition of success, so first we need to know what that tool is being used for. Check in on your big picture: what do you want to achieve? It doesn't need to be crystal clear; just jotting down a list of what feels important to you is enough. Grow your income? Increase conversion rates? Get more external opportunities? Be more visible? Introduce your new business? Pivot your offering? Secure your long-term growth? You may find it helpful to talk this through with a friend or use sticky notes and put a timer on to help yourself brainstorm. (Prompt to help with this: if you met the you of six months' time and deemed their marketing a success, what would be true?)

Reminder: Give yourself permission to connect to your vision – other people's definition of success isn't relevant here.

2. Action: Consider what you need to do with your marketing to achieve that result. This book will help you understand in detail how to achieve that result, but I want you to clarify an initial plan for how you'll make it happen. Do you want to be more consistent? Bring more personal content into the mix? Introduce platforms that aren't social media?

TIP
Set goals that stretch, but don't stress. I don't want you setting a goal so big that it feels intimidating and out of reach. I want your goal to stretch you to put in the work you otherwise wouldn't.

Summary / Action

Key learnings:

1. Marketing is simply a conversation where we use the buyer's journey to nurture a relevant community towards a sale.
2. Action needs direction, so having clear marketing goals will help you to take the right action with more ease.

Action steps:

- Explore your long-term vision and clarify one to three key marketing goals that feel important to you.
- Put your goal(s) somewhere visible. Whether it's as your laptop background or on your office wall, it's important to keep your vision front and centre.

2.
What is a marketing strategy?

I remember the first day I was asked about marketing strategy. I was seventeen years old, sitting in a meeting room in central London. I was asked if I could create a marketing strategy and, despite being wildly out of my depth and unsure what that really meant, I said yes. The eight-letter S-word instantly instilled fear in me. A strategy sounded complex, fancy and beyond anything I would be capable of creating.

Unsure of what to do, I made the obvious first step: Google. I typed in the phrase 'what is a strategy' and, bracing myself for a definition that just added to my overwhelm and fear, I was shocked at what a simple concept it turned out to be.

Alice Benham Dictionary
Strategy: an action plan with an end goal in mind.

Now, if we combine that with marketing, a marketing strategy is simply an action plan that helps you achieve your marketing goals.

It's not a complex spreadsheet.

Or a 48-page PDF.

It's simply a plan of action.

It's a plan that can look a million different ways and still be deemed successful.

You don't *need* a strategy, you *use* a strategy

I probably get one email a week including the phrase 'we *need* a marketing strategy' and it often makes me wonder – why?

The glorification and over-complication of the concept of strategy can lead us to want a strategy because... Because we should? Because it makes us feel good? Because that's what successful businesses do, right?

Wrong. Kind of.

You see, the goal isn't to <u>create</u> a strategy, it's to <u>use</u> one.

The purpose of a strategy is to help you take action. Not to make you feel good. Or take up space on your hard drive. Or impress your peers. It's to help you take action.

So, how about we simplify our definition of strategy and consider how we make them actionable, not fancy?

This whole book will revolve around that concept and unpack how we do it, but I quickly want to share what makes a strategy actionable so you can keep this in mind throughout:

- Make it actionable.
- Make it simple.
- Make it work for you.

The components of a marketing strategy

True to the mission of keeping strategy simple and actually useful, I want to introduce you to my three-step approach to marketing strategy. This is a framework I've developed over the last decade, used to help 10,000-plus business owners grow, and implemented within my own businesses. So I know it works.

Clarity + Plan + Action

These are three simple categories that make up an effective marketing strategy. Let's look at each of them in more detail.

Clarity

Before getting to the practical, we want to lay a foundation of clarity. It's very hard to create a plan if we don't know why it exists or who we're trying to reach, so this step is vital, yet often ignored. To create a marketing strategy, we want to get clarity on our goals, mission, messaging, target audience and brand. Once those are clear enough, it's onto the plan!

Plan

This is likely what you'll associate most with a marketing strategy, because it's where we get practical. Here we're defining our platforms and content; that is, where we are showing up and what we are showing up with. This step is all about getting specific with the 'how'. Rather than just doing stuff for the sake of it, here we are ensuring we make plans that are best suited to our goals.

Action

Last but definitely not least, we need to think about implementation. So often I see people create a shiny plan and completely ignore the question of how they will implement it. Many things can get in the way of us taking action, including lack of time or fear, so it's vital we put in the processes, habits and mindsets to help us take consistent action.

The whole of this book will follow this framework. By doing the same, you'll ensure you avoid the common mistakes I see people making and end up with a marketing strategy that actually works.

Strategies won't last forever

One of the biggest misconceptions many people have is that a strategy should be rigid and set. While we don't want to be changing our marketing strategy daily and giving our community whiplash, we do want it to evolve.

Your marketing is a direct reflection of your business, it's the voice of your business... and I bet your business changes over time, right? Whether you're changing your target audience by introducing new offerings or just seeing shifts in your industry or with people's buying behaviour, your marketing needs to evolve too.

The best marketing strategies are a constant work in progress. They're living, breathing things that we adjust over time.

I mean, can you imagine if no companies had evolved their marketing strategies to include the internet and now didn't have a website or social media?

Instead of aiming to create a marketing strategy that will last forever, aim to let it improve over time. Action breeds clarity, and the more you implement and show up, the more you'll learn. The more you learn, the more improvements you can make to your strategy.

Summary / Action

Key learnings:

1. A marketing strategy is simply a plan that helps you take action towards your business goals.
2. The three components to an effective strategy are: clarity, plan + action.
3. A strategy won't last forever. Let it evolve, and be open to learning from action.

TIP
To keep your strategy updated: have a 'CEO' day once a quarter where you check in with your goals, review previous progress and make any necessary changes to your marketing strategy.

3.
Don't sell to an audience, nurture a community

If there's one reframe I would like to get every business to understand about marketing it would be this: nurture a community, don't just sell to an audience.

So often when people's goal is to make sales, they assume the key is gathering the largest audience possible and delivering a sales pitch repeatedly until someone buys. That may work in the short term, but it isn't necessarily the most sustainable or effective approach.

In the past, the general approach to marketing has been this: stand on stage, shout a sales pitch to a crowd of people and hope somebody will take action. Think flyers, TV ads, cold calling... what I call megaphone marketing. I'm not saying that approach doesn't work, but we're already seeing that it won't cut it in years to come.

Consumers are changing.

They no longer want to just buy something; they want to feel a part of something. They want to love the brands and businesses they buy from. As competition grows, so does consumer choice, and the bar continues to be raised.

It's almost assumed now that you'll have a great product or service, so what else are you doing to stand out?

Consumers crave trust. They crave connection. They crave clarity on who they're buying from. They want to know your *why*, not just your *what*.

Put simply: they want community.

The sooner you listen to that, the sooner you'll begin to access this:

SELLING TO AN AUDIENCE	NURTURING A COMMUNITY
Anyone and everyone	Like-minded, relevant people
Buy once	Loyalty and repeat purchases
Look for the next cheapest competitor	Advocate for you
Just about selling and converting	Contribute ideas and suggestions
Short-term strategy	Long-term strategy

Fish prefer nets to rods

This is my favourite analogy for a community-first approach to marketing:

The traditional approach = cast your fishing rod into the big wide sea, hoping someone will bite but not giving any fish a reason to trust you.

A community-led approach = gather a small group of fish in a pond, nurture them with conversations (or fish food) that build their trust and relationship with you, and, when they're ready, simply pop in your net, inviting them to take action.

I don't know about you, but I prefer the net to the rod any day, both as a consumer and as a marketer. It just feels better.

Nurturing a community isn't just the most effective route to sales, it's the most value-driven approach too. If you ever find yourself feeling icky or uncomfortable around selling, it's likely because you were trying that old approach of shouting a sales pitch from a stage... so what if instead we sat you around a table to have a conversation with your people?

I bet that would feel more like the conversation that marketing really is.

I want you to hold that fish analogy in your mind whenever you approach your marketing. Who do I want in my pond? How am I bringing new fish in? What am I doing to nurture them? When and how do I pop the net in and invite them to buy?

Summary / Action

Key learnings:

1. Consumers are changing. They want to feel a part of something and know more than just your product or service.
2. Building trust is key to securing repeat and long-term sales.
3. Nurturing a community is the modern approach to marketing that will stand the test of time.
4. Discomfort around sales or marketing often comes from seeing it as a sales pitch rather than a community.

Action steps:

- Reflect on the brands you buy from. What do you like about them as businesses? How do they build community?
- Consider the ways you're following the traditional approach of shouting a sales pitch from a stage. How can you focus more on building a community?

Molly Masters of Aphra

I spoke with two entrepreneurs about how they've fostered a community-first approach and what tangible impact this has had on their business. Here's what Molly Masters, founder of literary brand Aphra, says about her experience and insights.

Was community building a focus you had from the start?

With a passion-led business, or really any business at all, the story and the community go hand in hand at the centre of your mission. In the early days, I posted what people wanted to see: book recommendations, reviews, competitions, quotes. I did everything I could to show up (despite feeling nervous on camera at first), and my community got to know my face. I felt incredibly proud that this year of just posting and growing really paid off. Just as authors love to share stories, bookworms inherently want to share the stories they have read and enjoyed, and Aphra gave them a space to do that as a community. I maintained this focus and the brand grew to the following of more than 200K it now has, while maintaining the feel of a small, intimate community.

What impact do you feel a community-first approach has had? Tangible results or examples are great.

The impact of a community-first approach has been nothing short of remarkable for Aphra. By prioritizing our subscribers and involving them in every step of our journey, we have fostered a deep sense of connection to our mission and products. It is incredible to witness how this approach has not only brought people together but also facilitated the formation of friendships and the birth of home book clubs. Moreover, our commitment to building a strong community has yielded significant tangible results for us. It has become a driving force behind our ability to secure partnerships and sponsored opportunities with larger businesses who recognize the immense value we have cultivated over the years. This recognition has positioned us exceptionally well for future growth.

What practical steps have you taken to build a community?

At the core of a meaningful community is value and connection. What a lot of people sadly get wrong at first on socials is going straight for the hard sell. I've done it; we all have! But you have to build a conversation and a

Left: Value-led content creates credibility and connection for a brand. 'The Chapters' is an entertaining podcast in which book lovers write in with dilemmas, and Aphra offers advice and the perfect book recommendations to see them through that chapter in their life.

Right: Sharing value-led content around the topics that relate to your business attracts and nurtures a community that is relevant to your product or service. Aphra consistently talks about the latest books in an engaging way to keep readers interested in its content.

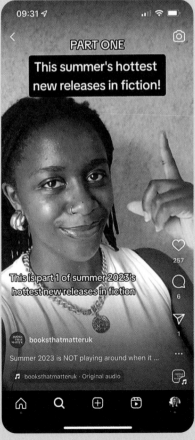

'The impact of a community-first approach has been nothing short of remarkable'

connection with your people, get them to trust you, understand why they should listen to what you have to say and take action from it. For me, it was getting underneath the questions of:

Why would people buy the books I recommend?

What is the problem they're facing and how can I show them I have the expertise and passion to solve it?

Who else are they listening to, and how can I be different, and better?

Starting the community with value-led content like book recommendations, reading tips and author bios was how we gained credibility with our book-loving followers. We turned them into a community by offering up more on other platforms, like a value-led podcast that is purely about answering our community's dilemmas and giving book recs, and having a weekly newsletter that goes out telling them all about the book world and releases they'll love. We also set ourselves apart by pairing with collaborators and brands they already love.

Any final tips for those looking to do the same?

To truly stand out from your competitors, it's essential to go beyond surface-level observations and dive deep into the customer experience they offer. Take the initiative to order their products, step into their shoes and conduct thorough analysis. But remember, the goal is not simply to copy what they're doing. Instead, leverage this knowledge to level up and provide something unique that sets you apart. By carefully studying your competitors and then surpassing their offerings, you can create a customer experience that is truly exceptional and positions your business as a leader in its own right.

Lauren Currie of UPFRONT

Lauren Currie is the founder and CEO of UPFRONT, an organization on a mission to support one million women with confidence, visibility and power. Here's why she's building a community-first business and how we can seek to do the same.

How do you define community?

I think that relationships are a currency and that's why communities have been the beating heart of every business I've built over the last 15 years. Community is more than just a concept: it's a fierce competitive advantage. I think it's similar to the transformative power of culture itself.

What impact has this approach had on your business?

I'm really proud of the impact our community-first approach has made. As the founder, the bond I share with our community is not just a connection, it's a source of energy, inspiration and motivation that fuels my entrepreneurial journey. Our data shows word of mouth is our strongest marketing channel – a testament to the quality of our product and the loyalty of our cherished customers: the 5,000 women who proudly call themselves Bonders.

The trust we've fostered with our Bonders is high, so this makes it easy to launch new ventures, learn from our mistakes and seek their invaluable input along the way. Their engagement, attentive listening and the grace they extend to us when we make mistakes all help us to build an amazing business.

What steps do you take to nurture community and how can others do the same?

My six top tips for creating community:

1. Vision: What is your community for? How will the world look different if you succeed?

2. Consistency: Show up. Be reliable and consistent in how you show up for your community, even if it's made up of five people.

3. Patience: Building genuine relationships takes time.

4. Choose your tool or platform: You can't be on all the tools. Choose the one that suits your purpose best.

5. Design your culture: You must set the tone of your community. If you don't, someone else will.

6. Doing not talking: Do something. Don't be a victim of inertia. Put yourself and your ideas out there. If your community flops, you've lost nothing.

But if you've stumbled across some untapped desire, people will find you. Your community will grow. You might even have the opportunity to monetize it, expand it, or at the very least improve your personal network.

Go start the group. Find others. Learn together.

'Community is a fierce competitive advantage'

Lauren and the UPFRONT community learning, celebrating and connecting at 'Upfront and Centre', the organization's very first in-person conference. Lauren explained, 'The palpable energy, the shared moments of connection, and the collective experience made for a day I'll never forget.'

4.
Knowing who you are and owning your greatness

If we're seeing marketing as a conversation, the first place we need to get clarity is in who we are. It's pretty tricky to have a conversation if you don't know who you're speaking as: kind of like if an actor were given a script but no direction on the character themselves.

As we touched on in the last chapter, nurturing a community is key. A huge part of that is connecting people to who we are, as businesses, as entrepreneurs and as organizations.

While it is tempting to hide behind your product or service, that approach won't cut it these days. Consumers are flooded with options, so why should they choose you over a competitor?

Put simply, your biggest USP is you: your mission, values, personality, impact, approach and story. This is why people choose your business. The clearer you get on that, the more you'll be able to bring it into your content and communicate it to others.

Say hello to your inner compass, the three components that make up who we are as businesses.

● Purpose ● Mission ● Values

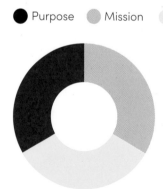

> **TIP**
> The clearer you are on who you are and why people choose you, the more confident you'll feel when showing up in your marketing.

I call it your inner compass because it should act like an internal north star: a central clarity that guides every decision you make – not just in a marketing sense, but in your business as a whole.

These three elements will be constantly evolving and clarifying, so whether you're filling in the blanks for the first time or revisiting this work, let's get into it.

PURPOSE: why do you exist?

'People don't buy WHAT you do, they buy WHY you do it.' Simon Sinek (*Start with Why: How Great Leaders Inspire Everyone to Take Action*)

A central part of building community is inspiring people with your vision. Connecting them to your why. Encouraging them to adopt your purpose as their own. That is why we need to know our why.

In business strategy we have two whys: an *internal* why and an *external* why.

Our internal why is why we run our businesses for us – the ways we want our business to complement and serve our lives. Although that part of why is very valid and key in business strategy, when it comes to marketing it's the external why that really matters.

Your community want to understand your why for them:

- Why do you do what you do?
- What is the purpose your business is led by?
- What's the story that led to where you are? What's your origin?
- What legacy are you aiming to leave?

MISSION: what do you do?

'So what does your business do?'

'Uh, so I kind of sell this thing that helps people who are a bit like this and yeah so... how about you?'

Feel familiar?

Whether the question is being asked by a distant relative at a family gathering, a panel host or a new face at a networking event, I often dread being asked what I do. Not because I don't like talking about business (far from that!), but because I struggle to explain what I do. Based on the conversations I've had with my community, I don't think I'm alone in that.

Explaining what we do should be simple, but because we're often so close to our own businesses, it can feel almost impossible to sum up. And when it comes to marketing, that's a big problem.

Put simply, if you're not clear on what you do, there's no way anyone else will be.

And if people don't know what you do, they can't buy. Confused people don't buy.

Clear external messaging begins with internal clarity. So often I hear businesses complaining that their messaging or content doesn't feel clear or compelling to others, it's confusing or overwhelming, and the source of that problem lies within.

Clarifying your mission is about more than just summing up the actual thing you do – photography, candles, brand design, life coaching – it's about going deeper than that.

You're not selling a thing; you're selling a transformation. The clearer you can get on that transformation, the more compelling your messaging will become. Here's an easy structure for us to follow to better understand our transformation:

Every product or service takes people on a journey, and understanding yours is key. So here are the three areas we want to get clarity in:

A: Problem or desire

Where are your clients or customers at the start of working with you or buying your thing? What are their questions? What are they feeling? What are their pain points and challenges? What are their desires?

When we understand this, we'll find it easier to create content that connects to these people and in turn begin to attract a relevant community. Effective marketing speaks to people before they're even ready to buy and helps them to identify their need for your offer. When we know what people are feeling or thinking at this stage, we can begin to do that.

B: Your offering and approach

The arrow between point A and C is your offering – the thing you sell or do that takes people on that transformation. It is a vehicle for change, in a way.

Being able to describe your product or service in a way that will make sense to everyday people may sound simple, but is often a skill we ignore as marketers. We jump straight to the strategic details without ensuring we can even describe what we sell.

This arrow isn't just about getting clarity on your 'thing' but also about what it actually does. This is especially true for service-based businesses, who I often find will overly focus on the title of their work. Here's what I mean:

- A brand designer doesn't just deliver brand assets and guidelines; they deliver a cohesive and strategic visual identity and insights around how it can be used.
- A life coach doesn't just deliver six hours of Zoom calls; they deliver the clarity, self-awareness and space people need to move forwards.
- A personal trainer doesn't just deliver weekly gym sessions; they deliver a personalized plan, specific feedback and accountability to stay on track.

So I want you to get clear on what you sell and what that actually involves. What do you offer that takes people on a journey?

C: Impact

This is the part of mission that many businesses get wrong: they don't define a compelling impact.

You see, people don't buy your thing because of what it is: they buy it because of what it means for them and the impact it'll have.

So often I see marketing that overly focuses on the format, when in fact it's the impact that will really draw people in.

Let's imagine I'm selling this book to you. I could use a couple of approaches:

1. Format-led approach: this book will be X pages and X words, walking you through the clarity plan and action phases of a marketing strategy. You'll learn expertise, be given action steps and read case studies and tips from other businesses.

2. Makes sense, but hardly speaks to you, does it? Now let's try an impact-led approach: this book will break down marketing strategy in a way that helps you take confident action towards your business goals. You'll be empowered with the simple expertise needed to stop guessing and start getting the visibility and sales you deserve. You'll leave feeling clear on your next steps, with a resource to come back to any time you need it.

I know which book I want to buy!

People buy impact, not format.

Of course, format is important. People need to know what it is they're actually buying, but let's ensure we know the impact too.
   Impact can look a lot of different ways depending on what you sell:

- How do they feel?
- What do they know?
- What are they able to do?

Knowing the impact that matters to *your* people is fundamental to writing copy and showing up in a way that converts.

Values: what do you stand for?

As consumers increasingly become conscious about the investments they're making, it's more important than ever to know and own our values.
   Your values are the 'how' of your business. They're what you stand for. They're how you want to be perceived. They should sit at the core of everything you do.
   A fun activity to try here is thinking about your business as a living, breathing person. What would they be like? How would people

describe them? What kind of person would they be at a party?

Defining three to five key values will not only help you feel more grounded in your business, but also breathe much more personality and depth into your content. The result? A more engaged community who want to buy from you, as proven by Sabira Silcock, founder of Sken Studios:

'One of our core values is sustainability, which we put into practice by making all of our jewellery from recycled silver and packaging them in recycled paper packaging. By filming myself working directly with recycled materials, I can be super transparent, allowing our customers to trust me both as a craftsperson, and also as a sustainable business owner. I know our customers' values mirror ours, so **whenever I share our sustainability efforts, we always receive positive feedback, which ultimately leads to sales.'**

You can't read the label when you're inside the jar

As you've read this chapter, you may have found some of these questions difficult or uncomfortable to answer. That's understandable, because we're basically trying to label a jar that we are within.

I remember first hearing the phrase 'you can't read the label when you're inside the jar' and immediately feeling like all my confusion around my business made sense. Of COURSE I found it tricky to quickly clarify my why, what and how... because they're within me.

If you find it easy to see other businesses clearly but your own feels foggy, you're not alone. I'm afraid I don't have a cure for this challenge, but I can offer some practical suggestions for helping you label the jar that you're within:

1. Change your environment and make time for it. This work requires a different headspace. It is best done when you have the time to properly step away from working 'in' your business and instead work 'on' it. Taking yourself to a coffee shop, going on a walk or setting aside a good few hours to get into this work will make this easier.

2. Do external research. Understanding the perspective of others who are outside the jar is invaluable, because they may be able to see your business clearer than you. Survey your community, speak to your past clients or customers or sit down with a trusted friend or coach. These external voices will likely kickstart your own clarity and help to confirm your assumptions.

3. Don't wait for it to be shiny or perfect. Our own businesses rarely feel really exciting to us, and that's normal. You're unlikely to reach a point of feeling like you've completed this work, because clarity is a constant work in progress. Know when it's good enough and remember that you can always revisit it down the line to refine and improve it.

Where to bring your identity

It's great knowing who we are, but the real impact comes when we inject this into our external action. The two primary ways we communicate our brand are through our voice and our visuals.

Voice

Both what you say and how you say it will connect your community to who you are as a business. Copywriter Ellie Kime has two great pieces of advice for nailing your tone of voice:

Drop the corporate voice
'Remember: personable doesn't mean unprofessional. You can be chatty and conversational and still be at the top of your game, doing incredible work – the idea that you can't is a relic of a bygone era.'

Talk, don't type
'If you find writing about yourself difficult, why not speak it? Use a dictation app to capture how you could explain what you do in

TIP
Find a business friend or like-minded person who can provide accountability, a space to process and some external support as you gain clarity.

person instead. Not only do you sidestep the blank screen panic and avoid censoring yourself, but you also document your actual, authentic tone of voice.'

Visuals

The visual identity of your business, from your logo and colour palette to fonts and photography, is a powerful way to communicate what makes your business unique.

I spoke with branding designer Liz Mosley, who shared that 'all of the aspects of your visual identity are tools to help consistently convey the right message about your business. Consider the personality that you are trying to convey when choosing fonts, photography and illustrations.'

For those feeling overwhelmed or unsure on where to start, Liz's top tips are:

Start with colours

'Colour is one of the first things people notice when it comes to your brand identity, so your colour palette is a great place to start and a way of drawing in the right people. Do you want to go for something whimsical and light or maybe dark and corporate? Colour is emotive so keep thinking back to how it will make your clients or customers feel and whether it will help you achieve your goals.'

Don't try to fit in

'Your logo is a really key part of your visual identity. It is almost like your brand's signature. You want to create something that's fairly simple and that stands out so people recognize your brand as quickly as possible. We are all bombarded with adverts from thousands of brands every day. If you design branding that authentically represents your business through all of the visual elements available to you, you can cut through the noise and create something memorable and distinctive.'

You can't
read the label

when you're
inside the jar.

Summary / Action

Key learnings:

1. Consumers don't just buy what you do, but also why and how you do it.
2. Internal clarity is key to being able to communicate your business in a clear and compelling way.
3. People buy impact, not format.
4. It's hard to read the label when you're inside the jar (that is, your business), so make time for this. Know that it's okay if it feels sticky at first and seek outside insight to help.

Action steps:

- Clarify your inner compass, reflecting on the prompts for your purpose, mission and values.
- Write out a mission statement that sums up your business. Try to capture what you do, how you do it and the impact of your product

5.
Who you're speaking to

Now we know who we're speaking *as*, it's time to clarify who we're speaking *to*. Imagine sitting down to have a conversation but not knowing who it's with... it would feel pretty impossible to know what to say and connect with the person, right?

Well, that's what happens when we don't understand our target audience.

When we know who we're speaking to, we're able to be much more specific with our plan. We can show up on platforms that we know are right for us. We can use messaging that is specific and speaks to the right people. And we can get much more intentional and effective when it comes to nurturing a community.

Your target audience will be unique to your business and your specific marketing goals. If you're trying to achieve sales, it will likely be your ideal client or customer. If you're growing your network and visibility, it may be other players in your industry. Check in with your marketing goals and ask yourself, 'Who do I need to reach to achieve this goal?'

Demographic versus psychographic

A lot of the time when people are encouraged to clarify their ideal client or customer, they're given a very specific way to do it: define a person. That is, create a persona that has a specific age, name, gender, location, income bracket and so on. While that can lead to a very specific-feeling target audience, I don't think it's particularly useful.

Let me demonstrate...

Only demographic

My stationery company, On Paper, sells productivity and organizational tools for business owners, freelancers and creatives. My ideal customer is:

- Called Bethany
- Aged 32
- Lives in London
- Has a sausage dog
- Shops in Zara
- Works freelance in design
- Takes home a 45k salary
- Holidays in Cornwall each summer

Now, not only does Bethany's life sound pretty good to me, she also sounds very specific. But the big question is: does this persona help me create content to sell stationery to Bethany? Not really.

I know who she is on a demographic level, but I don't find that list particularly inspiring or useful when it comes to marketing.

(The only exception I'll give is for paid advertising – understanding specific demographic traits can be necessary for targeted ads.)

The other thing to note is that this demographic-led approach forces me to get very specific and narrow about who I'm reaching. The customers for On Paper all have varying job titles, incomes, locations and personal habits, so why am I ruling people out just because I think I need to specify all these things to be 'good' at marketing?

Relevant demographic plus psychographic

That is why I'd suggest looking at the relevant demographic and *psychographic* qualities to define your target audience.

Knowing who you're speaking to is less about knowing what your community would tick in the census or write on their CV, and more about who they are under the surface. Their psychographic qualities are things like their:

- Interests
- Challenges
- Pain points

- Desires and goals
- Frustrations
- Values

So, if I defined On Paper's customers in this way I'd have a very different list:

- Work for themselves in some way
- Have ambitions to grow their business
- Struggle to stay organized and manage their time
- Want to spend more time working 'on' their businesses
- Value simple and effective tools

Now that's a list that I can use for marketing, because I've got something to work from that would help me create content that will connect with and serve those people.

I'm not saying demographics are entirely irrelevant, but I want you to think carefully about which demographic points are actually useful for your business. Maybe you want to reach a specific age bracket, gender or location – that's great, make sure to add that to your list, but please don't feel the pressure to make every area specific.

Defining a target audience is less about outlining one specific person and more about understanding a crowd of people and knowing what brings them together – the qualities they share.

I often notice we feel a resistance around speaking to a specific target audience, worried that will mean some people won't be interested in our work. And that is the goal.

We want to attract the people who are a great fit and gently repel those who aren't. If you try and speak to everyone, you'll speak to no-one. So give yourself permission to get specific and define the demographic *and* psychographic qualities that are true for your business.

How to know your target audience

You may be reading this and thinking, 'This sounds great, but I've got no clue on any of this, so where do I start with getting clarity?' I'm glad you've asked, because there are three key ways I'd suggest:

1 Reflect

Many of us start businesses because we ourselves experienced a problem or identified a gap in the market, so I bet there's some clarity already within you. If you identify with your ideal client or customer, consider what your answers to these questions would be.

2 Observe

Every piece of action we take gives us clarity back, so what can you learn from the past? Look at past client feedback, the type of customers you've sold to previously, sales and social media data, what people show you about themselves when you're in conversation with them and who is commenting on your competitors' content.

3 Ask

Nothing beats a good old survey! If you're building a community already, ask them some questions to help yourself better understand them. Or if you'd prefer to speak to past clients and customers or those in your network, reach out and get their insights. Sometimes we sit around thinking the answer is within us when actually we could just ask a few intentional questions to get instant clarity and confirmation.

If you're at the start of your business, be open to this getting much clearer over time. Action breeds clarity: the more time you spend connecting with people, the clearer you'll become on who you do and don't want to reach.

If you speak to multiple people, consider if you need to define multiple target audiences. If you're speaking to similar people but just with varying needs or at different stages on their journey, try to define a persona that sums everyone up. If you split it out and have multiple personas unnecessarily, you'll confuse your future self, who will then have to try and speak to three different people at once.

However, if you have very different target audiences (for example, you sell photography packages to couples getting married but also sell educational courses to new photographers), you will want to outline different lists for each. If the problem you're helping them solve is wildly different, splitting them out will make it clearer for you to understand how different parts of your marketing strategy are speaking to each of them.

Don't set it and forget it

It's very likely your target audience's thoughts and feelings will shift depending on what's going on in the wider world. Mako Ndoro runs Berry & Brie, the grazing table specialists, and puts time aside each month to stay connected to her customers' specific needs:

'People purchase with emotions that can be influenced by a variety of factors including political influence, social events, economic shifts and global pandemics. It's really important we stay aware and up to date with these influences in order to stay relevant and adapt to our clients' emotions and perspectives of buying during each phase of their emotions. My time is limited, so it is paramount that I set aside an allocated time at the end of the month to review our customer insights and stay clear on who we're speaking to.'

TIP
Your ideal client or customer may change as you launch new offerings, so make sure to check in with this work whenever you're coming up with new ideas.

Summary / Action

Key learnings:

1. Knowing who you're speaking to is key to specific, compelling and effective marketing.
2. It's important to be specific in who we're speaking to. If you speak to everyone, you'll speak to no-one.
3. Defining a very specific buyer persona can often lead to an unnecessarily narrow but also unhelpful piece of work.
4. Psychographic elements are the most valuable aspect to understand about your target audience.

Action steps:

- Carry out a research task to help clarify your target audience, whether that's reflecting on your own experience, analysing some past data or behaviour or sending out a survey.
- Define the psychographic and relevant demographic qualities that bring your target audience together.

6.
The buyer's journey

Now we've clarified our marketing goals, brand identity and target audience, there's one final and very important area for us to understand: the buyer's journey.

Alice Benham Dictionary
Buyer's journey: the process people go through from being strangers to your business to becoming clients or customers.

The goal of our marketing is to move people through the buyer's journey, towards a sale. So if we can understand the buyer's journey and how it relates to our business, we'll be able to approach marketing in a much more theory-led and clear way.

Back when I was 17 and totally new to the world of marketing, I took a number of online courses to help me develop my skills and make me feel less like an imposter. I clearly remember being on holiday in France with a friend and sitting outside our tent reading pages and pages about the buyer's journey.

The theory blew my mind. It helped me see marketing in such a clear way. It took away all the blue-sky thinking and vague advice I'd previously been frustrated by.

But the problem was, that theory was hidden within long, complicated definitions and overly fancy words. Business owners weren't accessing the impact of the buyer's journey because it wasn't said in words they could easily understand.

So began my mission to blend theory with action and teach marketing in a way that isn't only grounded in theory (and therefore much more effective) but is also easy to implement.

When we look at our marketing through the lens of the buyer's journey we can:

- Feel confident that the plan we're outlining will work for our goals.
- Be specific with the action we're taking.
- Stop doing stuff for the sake of it and confidently ignore advice that isn't right for us.
- Measure success clearly, knowing what we're trying to achieve.
- Actively bring people into our community and nurture them towards a sale, instead of just waiting for people who are ready to buy.

What is the buyer's journey?

'Alice, you've sold me on the benefits of knowing the buyer's journey, but please can we have a bit more detail?'

I'm glad you asked...

Everyone, when making a purchase, moves through the buyer's journey. It's the process of going from having a problem or desire to investing in the solution or fulfilment.

There are three key stages to understand:

Awareness > Consideration > Decision

1 Awareness

What's happening: they're not ready to buy, but they're experiencing a problem or desire and are ready to start exploring.

2 Consideration

What's happening: they're thinking about investing and asking the key questions:

- What is it?
- How does it work?
- Why should I get it?
- Do I want to buy it from these people?

3 Decision

What's happening: they're ready to buy and need the invitation or nudge to take action. They want the specific information and clear next steps.

> **TIP**
> Reflect on a recent investment you made and how you went through this buyer's journey yourself.

Traditional sales is about speaking to people once with a sales pitch and hoping either that they move through the whole buyer's journey in one swoop or that we've found them already close to the decision stage. Marketing is about speaking to people right from stage 1, giving them the information they need and gently nurturing them towards a sale.

Marketing with the buyer's journey in mind means you're always selling, but it never feels that way.

How marketing and the buyer's journey interact

The role of every touch-point within our marketing is to play a role in moving people through the buyer's journey. That's when this theory becomes useful: when we use it to inform the plans we make.

Let me break down what your marketing needs to do for each stage:

1 Awareness

EXPOSE: Connect with them, give value, help them to discover their desire for what you offer.

2 Consideration

NURTURE: Nurture them, connect them to us as businesses, show our products / services, demonstrate the impact.

3 Decision

CONVERT: Offer opportunities for people to buy with a clear call to action.

EXPOSE + NURTURE + CONVERT = Sales

Your marketing activity exists to fulfil that equation.

Pretty simple, right? It's okay if the actual implementation of that feels overwhelming (there's a lot of chapters to come that will help with that!) but for now, I want you to acknowledge the simplicity of that equation.

No fluffy advice.

No blueprints.

Just the three things to do to actively encourage sales, in a way that feels good.

Where's your weakness?

Whenever I talk people through this theory, my first question is always: which do you need to do more of?

As business owners, we all have strengths and comfort zones that result in weak spots and missing pieces.

- Perhaps you don't work to generate exposure with new audiences and speak to people right at the start of the buyer's journey.
- Maybe you're great at value content but rarely tell people what you do or give them the information they need to move through consideration.
- Or potentially you do stages 1 and 2 but don't ever invite action and ask for the sale, perhaps because it feels uncomfortable.

We're all imperfect human beings, so it's very natural to have an element within the buyer's journey we have more of an aversion to. Reflect on what yours might be and hold that close as we walk through the rest of the book – I want you to lean into the advice that will help you most.

Conclusion

Clarity is the foundation to an effective strategy, so now we've worked through your why, what, who and how, let's start creating your plan.

Remember: clarity is never 'finished', so know when you've got it clear *enough* and make sure to refine this work every few months or whenever your business changes.

Summary / Action

Key learnings:

1. The buyer's journey is the process people go through from being strangers to becoming clients or customers.
2. The three stages of the buyer's journey are awareness, consideration and decision.
3. When we understand our buyer's journey, we can create a marketing strategy with that in mind.
4. Based on the buyer's journey, the three things our marketing needs to do are expose, nurture and convert.
5. Every platform, content or piece of marketing action should play a role in moving people through the buyer's journey.

Action steps:

- Reflect on the buyer's journey for your business. What is your target audience feeling and thinking at each stage?
- Consider what you're currently doing to 'expose + nurture + convert' and reflect on which stage of the journey you're currently weakest at marketing to.

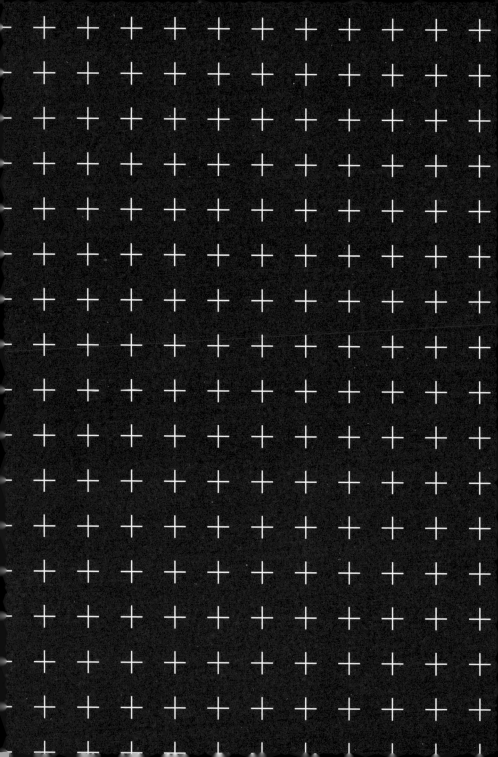

PART II
Create your plan

Platforms / Content

Platforms – where are you showing up?

Knowing where we're showing up and the various elements involved in creating a diverse marketing strategy is the first step to outlining our plan.

Let's outline which channels you're using and how they're working together to achieve your goals.

7.
How platforms fit together: exposure, nurturing, selling

Alice Benham Dictionary
Platforms: the various channels, touch-points and elements that work together to make up your marketing strategy.

Before we look at content and the details of marketing, we first need to define where we're showing up and, as importantly, *why* we're showing up in those places. In marketing it can be scarily easy to get 'shiny object syndrome', which is where we get distracted by new platforms, trends or ideas, thereby forgetting to commit to our initial plan. To help you avoid doing things 'just because', let's understand and identify what might be the right fit for you.

I want you to think of your marketing strategy as being like an ecosystem. Or a puzzle. Or a spider's web. Pick whichever analogy you like, but they all demonstrate the same point: it isn't about one thing doing all the work, but various elements connecting to each other and working as a team.

Your platform strategy should be a team effort, where each platform has a clear role to play in the buyer's journey.

Particularly with the rise in social media, it can be easy to fall into the trap of trying to have just one platform do all the work. Although that may get you results in the short term, it isn't the best approach because:

- You're putting all of your eggs into one basket – if that platform loses popularity or the algorithm changes, you'll be left with no marketing.
- You're not making the most of different platforms' strengths.
- You're only allowing for one way for people to find you (we want the most visibility possible, right?).

In short, a single-platform marketing strategy won't give you sustainable and efficient results, so that's why we want to create a multi-channel strategy. That sounds fancy, doesn't it? Don't be overwhelmed – it just means we're showing up in multiple ways in multiple places.

Five types of platforms

There are five types of platforms that we can have within our marketing strategy, each with its own strengths:

1. Website
2. Social media
3. Long-form content
4. Email marketing
5. Visibility touch-points

You don't necessarily need all of these platforms within your plan, but it's helpful to categorize them so we can understand the purpose they fulfil and decide if and when they're relevant for us.

Before we look at the buyer's journey, let's go through each platform in more detail:

1 Website

A central place where people can find key information about your business, be given next steps to buy or take action and also be directed to other platforms you may have.

2 Social media

An ongoing touch-point designed to discover new people, nurture community and point people towards your other platforms.

3 Long-form content

A content platform that takes people deeper, such as a blog, a podcast or a video series. You create longer content that connects people further to your mission, expertise and work.

4 Email marketing

A private space to nurture your most engaged community and invite sales.

5 Visibility touch-points

The elements you use to drive exposure: word of mouth, press, paid ads, networking, directories and so on.

Even from that brief outline, I hope you can begin to see why we want multiple platforms working together – because they all have different strengths. Your marketing strategy will be at its best when you choose platforms with a purpose. Not just because I want you doing less work if you can, but also so that when we get to figuring out the details of your platform, there's a clear intention already in place.

How they fit with the buyer's journey

As we've already seen, in order to move people through the buyer's journey we have to ensure we do three things:

EXPOSE > NURTURE > CONVERT

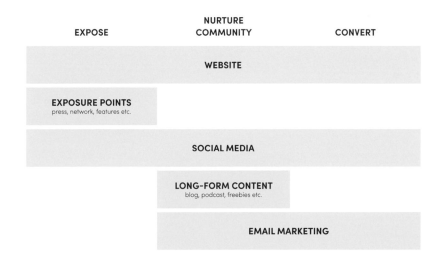

So let's look at how each platform serves our buyer's journey:

- Website: this can work for people at all stages. They should be able to come to your site and find information and next steps that are relevant for them.
- Social media: these platforms can do the full buyer's journey. Their biggest strengths are exposure and nurturing, but depending on what you sell, conversion can also be achieved here.
- Long-form content: these platforms will nurture your community effectively by connecting them to you, your work and your mission on a deeper level.
- Email marketing: the often unsung hero in the group, but this platform will be your best tool for nurture and conversion.
- Visibility touch-points: these elements work brilliantly at increasing your visibility and bringing more people in.

If you're already showing up, can you start to see how your current platforms may be working together to create a graphic like this? Use this section of the book to refine your approach and ensure you're using each platform in the most effective way.

If you're new to marketing, don't feel overwhelmed! You don't need to begin with all of these platforms in place. I'd rather you begin with one or two platforms, do them well, build the muscle and then diversify from there. If I can save you some hassle in trying to work it out, I'd suggest beginning with a website, one social platform and email marketing. Then add more into the mix.

TIP
If you're ever feeling lost with your marketing, listing out your platforms and what goal they each help to achieve will give you an immediate sense of direction.

Summary / Action

Key learnings:

1. Our platforms should work together like an ecosystem, each having a clear role.
2. There are five main types of platform: website, social media, long-form content, email marketing and visibility touch-points.
3. We should look at our platforms through the lens of the buyer's journey and understand their purpose. Are they for exposure, nurturing or conversion?

Action steps:

- Map out your current platforms, reflecting on the role they're currently playing within your marketing strategy.
- Define your ideal platform strategy, adding in the platforms you feel are missing or that you'd like to introduce.

8.
Creating an impactful website

A website can work really hard within a marketing strategy – is yours?

When you start a business, 'create a website' is often regarded as a tick-box exercise. It shows up on almost all of the 'what to do when starting a new business' lists online. As a result, it can be something we do and then abandon.

The role of a website in your strategy

The most common mistake I see people making is seeing their website just as a place where people can buy. Of course, a website is typically a place where people purchase your product or enquire about your services, but that doesn't have to mean that's its only purpose.

Bringing this back to our buyer's journey, your website has the capacity to facilitate every stage:

- It can drive visibility through SEO and give those new to you some valuable content (exposure).
- It can nurture your current community by educating them on who you are and connecting them to other platforms (nurture).
- And, of course, it can help people take the next step and buy (convert).

A hard-working website does all three of those things: it acts as a central space where anybody can find a piece of relevant information and a next step to take.

I'm curious: if I were to go to your website right now, would you feel confident that it would accurately reflect your business and give me the most up-to-date information? If the thought of me doing that makes you uncomfortable, that's a sign your website could be doing more for you.

You don't need a website... but why wouldn't you?

In the past I've got into debates with people who don't feel they need a website, either because they sell through other channels or perhaps don't need the functionality of a website to make sales, or they decide it's a fluffy extra that will waste their time to create.

To them (and in fact everyone) I say – you don't need a website, but why not have one?

A website is the one platform where you have ultimate autonomy.

So many other platforms come with algorithms and boxes we have to squeeze our message into, so isn't it time we had a platform that we owned and had complete control over? How about we take advantage of what a great tool your website can be.

Creating a sitemap

Whether you're editing a site you already have or starting from scratch, you want to begin with your sitemap. This is an outline of the pages and key information you want your website to communicate.

Especially if we're doing our own website, it is easy to be distracted by the visuals and focus overly on the way the site looks before we have the content nailed. Visuals are important, but the right content is the foundation to an effective website. After all, there's no use it looking great if it doesn't actually contain the right information.

The number and types of pages totally depends on what you want your website to achieve. So that's a good question to ask yourself first: what do I want from my website?

Imagine all the people who may be visiting and consider the information you want your website to communicate to them and the next steps you could encourage them to take. For example, someone totally new to you may be looking for some free expertise and a link to join your mailing list. A potential customer may be looking for FAQs and to check out. A journalist or an industry professional may want to learn more about your backstory or current features.

Start with a list of content, then begin to organize that into pages. If I can give you a head start, this is a pretty typical structure:

Home: the central landing page, this acts as a top-line intro to your business and sends people to the individual pages.

About: connects people to you as a business – communicates your story, mission, values and achievements.

Services/Shop: outlines your offerings (remember: features and benefits), key information and the next steps to buy or enquire.

Content: serves your visitors through a blog, link to your podcast, free resources or newsletter sign-up.

Contact: shares your contact details and an enquiry form if that's a right fit.

You'll also need the legal pages such as T&Cs and Cookies Policy, along with any other pages that are relevant for your business, such as Case Studies, FAQs or Meet the Team.

Per page, I'd suggest making a bullet-point list of content to include, again asking the question: what do the people coming to this page want?

That sitemap will help you spot any content gaps. You can then begin to create or edit your website with a plan already in place.

TIP

Write your website copy away from your website builder. Your brain will get distracted by the visuals, so write your copy in a document. Only once you're happy with it, drop it into your website and do the design.

Creating a journey

Instead of seeing your website as many individual pages, you want to look at it like a journey you're creating, where the pages link up to take people through the site. Our use of social media and phones has made us scrollers not clickers, which in the context of a website means we should always be giving people next steps.

Here are two ways to ensure you create a journey through your website:

1 Use your home page to signpost to other pages

Your home page will most likely be your most visited page, so ensure it works as a signpost to other more specific pages. Use banners to introduce key topics and then include a clear link that will take people through to that topics page. For example, do a short intro to your story and then link to your About page for people to find out more.

2 Never have a dead end

The end of every page should include a link to another page. Consider what the best next step would be. For example, if I've just read your About page, maybe it's time for me to read your services page. If I've just read your services page, perhaps I'll want to contact you. Never leave it up to the user to find their next step; make it clear and obvious to them.

Quick tips for a great website

Start with an intro

The top section of every page is your most precious real estate. It's what everyone will see and use to decide if they want to keep scrolling. This is most true with your home page, so use this space wisely! Ensure it grabs attention, gets to the point and introduces people to your business.

Type like you talk

A website is a reflection of you and your business, so make it sound that way! It's jarring to go to someone's website and feel like you're hearing from a corporate robot, especially when they're not like that in other content or in real life. Write copy that sounds and feels like you. Remember: the goal is to communicate and connect, not to impress.

Link it to your other platforms

Your site should be a central part of your marketing strategy, which both points to other platforms and is directed to from there. Does your website give me links to your other platforms? And how frequently are you sending traffic to your website from those platforms? The more links you create, the more all of your platforms will grow.

TIP
Even if a professional is building your website for you, ensure they use a platform that makes it easy for you to add your own edits down the line.

SEO

Doing your own SEO can feel overwhelming, so I spoke with Charlotte Klitgaard, SEO expert and founder of Wild SEO Agency, to get her top tips.

Alice Benham Dictionary

SEO: search engine optimization, also known as building a website that shows up on Google and gets you in front of new and ideal audiences.

Know your audience

Use language in your pages, blogs, menus and buttons that your audience would use themselves. It will help them find you on search.

Mobile first

Search engines look at mobile versions of websites before desktop versions, so ensure your site is designed well for mobiles and easy to use for fingers and thumbs.

Page-to-page links

Internal linking is vital for both people and robots to navigate their way around your website. Wherever relevant and possible, include a link to somewhere else on your own site.

Design your website as a user

Make it easy for your audience to complete calls to action in as few clicks and as few pages as possible.

Use free tools to enhance your website

There are many tools available like Google Search Console and Lighthouse Developer that give insights and specific recommendations on how to improve your site for search. Use them.

Visuals

Once you've nailed your copy, it's time to think about design!
I spoke with brand designer and strategist Eva Couto to discover
how we can create a great-looking website ourselves.

Brand identity before website
Designing an impactful website starts with having a great brand
identity to apply to it consistently. Figure out your colour palette,
logo and type suite beforehand and you'll find the design process
a whole lot smoother.

Break it up
Most people scan headings and highlight text to form their first
impression, so make sure your visitors aren't getting lost (or bored)
in a wall of text. Break up your copy often and use different
headings (H1–H5, and paragraph text) to differentiate between
what we should read first, second and so on.

High-quality but small images
While high-quality photos, videos and animations are great tools
to create visual interest and make visitors stick around your website
longer, they also take up a lot of space. Plus a slow-loading photo
can lose a user's interest. Before adding these to your website,
make sure they're as compressed as possible without losing quality
and opt for embedded code when you can.

Don't forget about mobile devices
There's nothing more annoying than opening a link to find a website
with ridiculously small type, buttons and icons so tiny you can't get your
finger to click the right spot or an empty horizontal scroll that leads
to a white wall. Remember that 55% of users – over half – will see our
website through their phones, so check it works for a mobile screen.

Consider accessibility and inclusivity
Check WCAG (Web Content Accessibility Guidelines) and pay attention
to colour contrast for those who might have different types of colour
blindness, use alt text for images that can be read aloud by screen
readers and include assistive technologies compatibility.

Summary / Action

Key learnings:

1. A website is working hard for you if it offers information and next steps to every stage of the buyer's journey.
2. Your website offers an unparalleled opportunity for you to create a digital storefront that you own and can communicate what you want, how you want.
3. Outlining a sitemap of pages and content is the first step to creating or improving a website.
4. Avoiding dead ends will help you create a journey throughout your site and link your pages up.
5. Search engine optimization can be achieved through small and considered edits to your content.
6. Ensuring your website looks good and can be navigated easily on mobile is key.

Action steps:

- If you already have a website, get someone else to look through and audit it. Ask them if it's clear what you do.
- If you're starting a new website, outline your sitemap and draft the copy away from your website builder.

9.
Harnessing the power of social media

Social media is something many of us have a love/hate relationship with when it comes to marketing ourselves or our businesses. In the last ten years we've seen it go from being a fluffy extra within marketing strategy to something almost everyone has as a core part, whether that's global brands or solo entrepreneurs.

When I reflect on my own relationship with social media as a business owner, I feel immense gratitude. It is without a doubt one of the biggest ways my business has grown over the years. I can confidently say I wouldn't be doing the work I do now without it. Heck, I likely wouldn't be writing this book without it.

My clients and friends would say the same. Networking. Learning. Connecting. Building community. Selling.

But like most things in business, it can present challenges too. I've both experienced and witnessed how social media can be a real source of frustration and difficulty for business owners when used in the wrong way.

So, is it an incredible tool for growth or a pit of comparison and time wasting? I say it can be both... so your experience of social media depends entirely on how you approach it.

A lot of the advice out there is to 'just show up' or 'create consistent content'. Although that's great, it's lacking in context. With this chapter I hope to help you better understand how to approach it in an intentional way.

Why use social media?

The first step to intentional social media marketing is knowing why you're using it. Action without purpose is a recipe for inconsistency and frustration, so let's begin there.

I'll never say that you *need* to use social media, but I hope I can deliver a pretty solid case as to how it would benefit you and your business. Here are the big seven benefits of social media:

1 Grow your sales

We may as well start with the big one: making money! Social media can be an incredible way to increase your sales and scale revenue. Content alone can help you find new audiences, generate leads, move customers into a sales funnel and encourage repeat purchases.

2 Increase your visibility

As people continue to use social media as search platforms, there's no denying it: the more visible you are, the more opportunities you'll be open to. Whether it's winning awards, featuring in press or even getting a book deal(!), being visible on social media will get more eyes on you.

3 Build community, not customers

We all know that word of mouth is marketing gold, so why not use social media to nurture your brand fans? By rewarding their engagement and connecting with them on a more personal level, you'll build a community who rave about your work as much as you do.

4 Stand out against the competition

As markets become more saturated, your biggest USP is you. People don't just buy because your product or service is great; they buy because of your story, values, approach and personality. And social media is the perfect platform to show those things off!

5 Raise your profile as an expert or founder

Building your own personal brand is an incredible way of getting more eyes on your work and getting cool opportunities like speaking gigs and press features. There's no better place to do that than on social media.

6 Network

It's not what you know, it's who you know, right? While I'd argue that statement is a little dramatic, the sentiment rings true: your network is important. Knowing key people in your industry will generate more opportunities, and having business friends around you will give support when you need it most.

7 Learn

Last, but absolutely not least – social media is an incredible tool for learning. Consuming valuable content, being inspired by what other businesses are doing and gaining data from your customers will empower you to grow.

Oh – and did I mention all of that can be achieved for <u>free</u>, without the need for <u>any</u> expensive equipment?

You may see how social media could deliver you all of those benefits, or just a couple might be important to you. Either way, I'd really encourage you to take a moment, look at the above list and ask yourself: **why am I using social media?**

The more connected you are with *why* you're using it, the easier you'll find it to take the right action, push through the challenges involved and measure your success.

Not yet sold on social media? Flip to the end of this chapter for a case study that will convince you otherwise!

I won't mention the algorithm... again

You may expect a chapter about social media to be littered with chat about the dreaded algorithms, which, if you don't know, are the systems that decide how, when and whether your content is seen by people.

There's a lot of content out there about how to 'beat' the algorithms or 'cheat' the system. While I'm sure some of it contains valuable insights, I don't think that's where our focus should be.

Yes, it's frustrating when a platform changes and we have to adapt...

Of course I sometimes wish we could keep doing the same thing...

And sure, it would be nice if the bigwigs at Facebook helped us reach more people for free...

But let me give you some tough love here: social media companies don't owe us anything. Although it would make sense for them to listen to what their users want, ultimately, we're using their tool, *for free,* to grow our businesses. Sure, we'll need to adapt over time as the platforms change, but that isn't so bad in exchange for the free potential, is it?

Instead of getting frustrated or perplexed by the algorithms, I want to offer you a different perspective:

- We're connecting with people, not beating algorithms.
- We should be constantly adapting our marketing to the change, seeing this evolution as a sign we're staying relevant.

You up for ditching the algorithm chat and focusing on using social media for connection? Okay, great; glad we're on the same page.

Now we're clear on *why* we're using social media, let's get into the details. Chapters 10–13 contain a lot of relevant tips and insights around the details of using social media, so here we're going to focus on the basics, because often it's the basics that we're getting wrong.

Choosing the right platforms

With so many platforms out there and a new one that 'you just HAVE to be on' appearing every few weeks, it can be hard to know where to show up. That can either lead to being on none or, in some cases, trying to be on all of them.

If the latter resonates, I'd really encourage you to narrow your focus. Running a business is hard enough without seven different channels to create content for. Most of the time, when we try to do everything we end up doing nothing.

Start with one or two platforms that make most sense for your business and do them well. Give yourself the time needed to show up consistently and strategically and you'll see results far quicker than if you half-arsed four platforms.

Then, if/when you have the resources to create more and can see the benefits of doing so, you can diversify.

So how do you know which platforms make sense for you? There are three things to consider:

1 Where is my audience?

If the people you're trying to reach aren't there, don't use it. Not sure where your audience is? Do some research: look at where your competitors are, stalk your ideal audience or ask them directly where they connect online.

2 Which makes sense for my message and style of content?

If you want to create visual and video content, Twitter may not be for you, so how about Instagram or TikTok?

3 What will I enjoy using?

This may sound trivial, but if you're choosing between two very similar platforms, go for the one you're drawn to! Enjoying it will make you more consistent and create higher-quality content.

Setting up your profiles for success

So you've chosen a platform, what next? It's time to create your profile – or, if you're already established online, to optimize your profile.

The beauty of social media is that you can change your profile over time, so while you don't need to put too much pressure on this, there are a few things to consider.

TIP

If you know your ideal audience is still on other platforms, you could still have a profile and ensure it links to your website, so it acts as a landing page for anyone searching for you.

Tell people what you do

This may sound obvious, but I frequently visit someone's page to learn more and leave still not being sure what they actually do. Make sure your bio or About section clearly explains what you do, who it's for and the impact of your product or service. Oh – and make sure it's in words your ideal customer will actually understand!

Make it personal

Social media is built for people, not businesses. As tempting as it can feel to hide behind your logo or corporate jargon, make sure to use images of you, put your name on there and tell people about who you are! Remember, that's your biggest USP.

Give a call to action

If I visited your social media right now, would I find a link to your website or a next step that you want me to take? People can only do something if we invite them to, so put a link to your product, newsletter or podcast.

The equation to social media growth

If you search online for 'social media marketing tips', you'll come across thousands of different 'secrets', 'hacks' and 'must-use strategies' for growth. Now, I don't doubt that many of those tips are valuable, but I'll say that:

1) nothing is a secret to growth, and
2) there's one formula that underpins it all.

If you take one thing from this chapter let it be this:

Consistent valuable content + engaging with your audience + learning and adapting = growth

That's it. There are three pivotal steps to growing your brand on social media. Let's break them down...

1 Consistent valuable content

Content is the foundation of social media. Whether it be in the form of video, text, audio or photo, one thing stays the same: value is key. Being informative, inspiring, relatable and entertaining in a way that's relevant to your target audience will be the key to convincing them to both follow and stick around. Oh, and you have to do it consistently! In the same way that one brick doesn't build a house, one piece of content doesn't generate success.

2 Engaging with your audience

Social media shouldn't be a one-sided conversation, so instead of 'posting and ghosting' make sure to engage back. Respond to your audience, reach out to interesting people and make time for using social media as it was intended: to connect.

3 Learning and adapting

No social media strategy will last forever, and it shouldn't! Sustainable long-term growth comes down to analyzing your data, learning from experience, noticing the changes and adapting your strategy to suit. An openness to evolving is key if you want to stand the test of time on social media.

There's a lot more detail we can go into, from content that sells and harnessing video to planning your marketing and choosing metrics, but that's what the later chapters are for.

Avoiding the traps and challenges

As mentioned right at the start of this chapter, social media is an incredible tool when used intentionally. It can allow us to access growth and opportunities unlike any other marketing platforms, but it also has its challenges: Comparing ourselves to others, getting wrapped up in the numbers, wasting precious time online...

If those resonate with you, first I'd say: you're not alone. I regularly find myself falling into those social media traps; don't think you're a bad marketer or business owner if you do too. They're things we need to be aware of and try to avoid, so here are a few reminders to help you:

Comparison

Social media bombards us with the highlights reels of others. Sometimes that can offer a source of inspiration, but sometimes it can be detrimental to our own progress or our mental health.

- Unfollow those who don't spark joy (hello, Marie Kondo!) or mute accounts if you just need a break from their content.
- Curate your feed intentionally. You choose the newspapers you read carefully, so treat your feed in the same way.
- Remember that while you only get to see the shiny stuff, there's a lot going on behind the scenes that you don't know about.

Vanity metrics

It's all too easy to start seeing social media as your business and directly equate your success and self-worth with your follow number.

- Know and remind yourself of the metrics that really matter: profit and sales.
- Put social media in its place: it's a tool for growth, not the definition of your business.

Time wasting

Our time is precious and social media can suck up a scary amount of screen time.

- Bring in boundaries. Try picking certain times in the day when you do or don't use your phone, setting limits on your social media apps and moving your phone away from yourself if you're in focus mode.
- Enter with intention. When opening an app, ask yourself 'Why am I going online right now?' Is it to post, engage with others or mindlessly scroll for the next hour to avoid your work?

None of us will ever be perfect at avoiding these traps, but the more aware we are, the better we can help ourselves in future. Check in with yourself; ask: 'How can I make my use of social media joyful and healthy?'

Summary / Action

Key learnings:

1. Social media is an incredible tool for increasing sales, brand and visibility. But remember that social media is a tool, not a measure of success.
2. It's important to know why you're using it, so you can show up with intention.
3. You'll never 'beat' the algorithm, so focus on building community instead.
4. Being on fewer platforms but with more energy and consistency is often better than trying to be everywhere.
5. The only 'secret' to growth is consistent valuable content + engaging + adapting and learning.
6. Social media can have its dark sides, so curate your feed and consume with intention.

Action steps:

- Set an intention for your use of social media: what goals do you want it to achieve?
- Reflect on which platforms are right for you.
- Optimize your profiles – are they clear and personal, and do they include a call to action (CTA)?
- Find people to follow who inspire you and may be relevant for your network.

Sasha Gupta of Cheeky Zebra Cards

Curious to hear some real results of what harnessing social media can do for you? I spoke with my client and friend, Sasha Gupta of Cheeky Zebra Cards, to unpack her story with social media – her results, challenges and lessons.

Where did you start with social media?

I first began showing up on social media in 2018 as a tick-box exercise, thinking it was just the thing you did if you had a business. I was following blanket advice, making no sales through content and on the whole finding it quite stressful. Driven by frustration and a desire for growth, I started taking it seriously at the end of 2019, beginning by setting the goal to build a memorable brand and start seeing sales as a result.

Did the growth come quickly?

It took six months of consistent action to see the right results, like engagement from my audience, repeat customers, people actually knowing who we are. In the early days I had to use others' success as my motivation and keep reminding myself that action was the best way to learn and improve. I remember the first person saying, 'I always buy my cards from you' and in that moment me realizing that it was actually working!

How has social media impacted your business?

Social media has saved my business. We used to rely on paid ads to achieve sales, but as a result of our community we've got more organic sales and, as a result, higher profit margins and a more diverse and sustainable approach. In 2019 we made less than £100 through social media and now it's over £100,000!

We also now reach millions of new customers each month through viral content and have been able to grow a relevant email list of 25,000-plus buyers.

As platforms and content change, how do you stay current?

A diverse strategy will ensure you're not relying on one platform, which makes it less of a panic when algorithms and user behaviours change. I like to keep my ear to the ground when it comes to marketing trends and what's working well for others, by listening to podcasts or connecting with other small business owners. And I embrace new things! Each time I plan a launch I commit to testing something different, to ensure I'm always experimenting and learning.

Any top tips for other businesses wanting to succeed on socials?

Stop thinking everyone else is smashing it. I struggle with a lack of resources, find social media tiring, forget to check my metrics and get caught up in follower numbers or mean comments just like you!

Have the right systems and processes. This saves you so much time and headspace with your marketing. I plan content and batch create content in advance, to ensure any last-minute emergencies or mindset wobbles don't get in the way.

Stop overthinking it and just take action. One of my posts will get 200 views and the next one will have 1,200,000. Imagine if I'd given up because the first one didn't perform well.

Opposite left: By clarifying her message, consistently sharing valuable content and engaging with her community, Sasha has built a committed and profitable following on Instagram, which rivals her high-street competitors.

Opposite right: Finding unique ways to incorporate products into social content means that Sasha's community is being sold to without it feeling icky or salesy.

Below left: People buy from people, so sharing your behind-the-scenes with your audience is a simple yet powerful way to build recognition and loyalty. Sasha regularly documents the day-to-day running of Cheeky Zebra.

Below right: Instead of using social media as a highlights reel, Sasha shares both the highs and lows with her following. This type of content keeps the viewer interested and builds their trust in the brand.

Packing the last order of the day

A day in the life of a famous candle maker

Consistent valuable content + engaging with your audience + learning and adapting

= growth.

10.
Creating long-form content

Ever listened to a podcast or read a blog? Then you've consumed long-form content!

I define long-form content as anything that goes deeper than a social media post. As the name suggests, it's a longer piece of content that can complement a surrounding marketing strategy brilliantly.

You're ready for long-form content if...

You're showing up on social media but feel a level of depth is missing

One of my biggest frustrations with social media is the way we're forced to fit our message into a pre-defined structure. We're often limited by how much we can say, either by the platform itself or because we know it won't get the same reach because people's attention span is limited there. It can sometimes feel like the more nuanced or detailed conversations we want to have don't really work there.

Enter long-form content! A space with much more time and length available to you, where the need to compete with other content is removed and you can share what you want in a way that feels right to you.

You're a service-based business and want an opportunity to share your expertise

The best way to nurture people towards a sale is to give them a taster of what they're buying, and that's exactly what long-form content can provide. Whether you're an educator, a mentor, coach or strategist, sharing your insights and perspective will increase prospective clients' trust with not just your expertise, but you as a provider too!

One of my favourite things about podcasts and videos is how easy they make it to show your personality. If you resonate with being stronger at talking than typing, you may find a home using long-form content.

You're a product-based business and want to build more community connection and impact through content

If nurturing community is one of your marketing goals, long-form content will help you start conversations that are related to, but not overly focused on, your product. Whether you're a beauty brand starting a blog of skincare tips, a book subscription business hosting a podcast interviewing authors, or a stationery company filming videos around productivity, long-form content allows you to serve your community in a whole new way.

You already have visibility elsewhere and are missing a next step for people

While I'm a big fan of long-form content (can you tell?), its one weakness is visibility. While it's not true for all, some types don't have an easy way for new people to discover them.

Take a podcast, for example; the only chance of people discovering it organically is if they search for a term that's in the title (somewhat unlikely) or one of the big streaming platforms features it on the home page (incredibly unlikely). Because of this, it makes sense to introduce long-form content when we already have visibility elsewhere.

Whether it's from social media, ads or PR, if there are already eyes on you and you want to create a next step for that traffic, long-form content can work well.

The exception to this rule is blogging, which can do wonders for your SEO.

Maddy Shine, a visibility expert, says: 'Blogging is the easiest way for any small business to get to page one of Google results and be found by new audiences. Google is a huge source of information and will promote the websites that produce *useful* information, a style of content that is most easily presented in blogs because they're easy to read and more up-to-date than a regular page of your website. Top tip? Check out Google's "People Also Ask" section when you Google your products or services. You'll find four easy questions you can turn into four easy-to-write blogs that are relevant to your audience. Ta-dah!'

The importance of linking it up

One of the biggest challenges we face in marketing is the level of content creation we have to keep up. Our time is limited, so how can we make it easier for ourselves to show up consistently?

Enter long-form content.

One of my favourite benefits of creating something long-form is that you can then use that content to help populate your other channels. There are two main ways you can do this:

1 Let long-form take the lead

If you're regularly sharing a long-form piece of content, one approach you can take is to let that idea become the leading theme across all your channels. That way you're not scrambling to come up with four ideas for four different platforms, but can link them all together.

For example, if I shared a podcast episode next week about 'five things I learned writing a business book', that could set the theme of 'writing my book' for other channels. I could share some behind-the-scenes videos on Instagram, talk more about how I got the deal via my emails and share some tips for others wanting to write a book on LinkedIn. By letting the podcast episode set the theme I've taken away the need to come up with more ideas and given my other platforms an instant intention.

2 Repurpose your long-form content

Another brilliant way to get more out of your long-form content is to repurpose it elsewhere. Repurposing is the action of recycling one piece of content and adjusting it slightly to work on another platform. Using that same podcast episode example, here's a few ways I could do that:

- Create a graphic rounding up the five lessons.
- Cut up the recording and share each lesson individually as a video.
- Post the video on my blog and YouTube to drive more traffic and visibility.
- Transcribe the recording and turn it into multiple captions for social media.

That way I've created one piece of content, but from that gained ten-plus more pieces of content.

These tips are great not just to save yourself time and headspace, but also to ensure people are moving between your platforms.

Remember: your marketing strategy is more effective the more you link your platforms up. By creating content that complements other platforms and reminding people to go over to X platform for more, you're making it clear and easy for your community to connect with you elsewhere.

TIP
When you plan long-form content, already be thinking about how you may want to repurpose it elsewhere. This will ensure you create it in a way that lends itself to being cut into other pieces of content.

Summary / Action

Key learnings:

1. Long-form content is anything that allows you to take up more space than a social media post: podcast, blog or video.
2. This style of content performs very well as a way of taking an audience deeper and building community.
3. You can use your long-form content to save you time with other content by repurposing and linking it up.

Action steps:

- Reflect on what role a long-form content platform could play in your marketing strategy.
- If you already have a community, ask them about what they want more of from you and which platform may suit them best (podcast, video, blog, etc).

Alice Benham of Starting the Conversation

I wanted to add a case study in here to demonstrate the power of long-form content and was thinking, 'Okay, my podcast has been the BEST thing I've done marketing-wise. Who could I interview who has done something similar?' Then I realized it was okay to just share my own experience.

This will be a self-interview, so bear with me while I wrap my head around how to do it...

When and why did I start my podcast?

I began the podcast back in 2018 as a way of educating people on what it takes to start and run a business. I was very young myself and had found my first few years of business to be a rollercoaster of opportunity and challenges, so I was passionate about both inspiring others to explore alternative careers and normalizing the tough stuff that happens behind the scenes.

What impact has it had on me and the business?

My business wouldn't be where it is today without the podcast, and I can say that with total confidence. It's allowed me to build a far deeper connection with my community than any social posts could, to sell to potential clients in a really gentle and value-driven way, to build my network and make friends just by inviting people on and to give me a platform to grow my confidence as an expert. Most of the opportunities I get – press, speaking, this book, even (!) – have been helped by the podcast in some way.

It also gives me a lot of security knowing that if social media went down or drastically changed, I'd have another way to easily reach my community.

What has the podcast taught me about long-form content?

That it can take time for content to start performing how you want it to. The podcast took over a year to gain traction. While I blame part of that on my rubbish promotional skills back then, I do notice long-form content being a slow burner sometimes.

Let me put it into numbers: we get the same average downloads in a day after five-plus years as we did in a month in that first year. When I say barely anyone listened bar me and my mum, I mean it!

But I'm glad I didn't give up. I loved the concept. I knew it had legs. So I just stayed consistent and improved as I went.

Tips for starting a podcast

1. Love your concept: Podcasts take a lot of time and consistency to work, so you've got to be excited about what you're creating.

2. Start messy: You'll never feel ready and likely not begin with a fancy studio or incredible quality, and that's okay! Start with what you know, start with what you have, and trust that you'll learn best through action.

3. Promote it: It's easy to assume people know your podcast exists because you know it exists, but you have to be repetitive in your promotion. Share it on socials, talk about it when you're networking. People can't listen if they don't know it exists.

4. Be okay with investing in it: Podcasts are hard to get direct revenue from, but that's not what it's about. The biggest gains you'll get from a podcast are indirect ones, so don't expect to see immediate financial payback; measure the qualitative results and ensure you have the time or budget to commit to it consistently.

ALICE BENHAM

STARTING THE
CONVERSATION

11.
Getting the most from email marketing

Writing a book on marketing is a little scary, I won't lie, partly because I'm talking about topics, strategies and tips that could be totally irrelevant in years to come. Marketing, particularly digital marketing, is one of the fastest-evolving parts of business, and none of us really know where things will be in five, ten or twenty years.

Although there's one exception to that statement.

There's one chapter I never worry will become irrelevant.

Only one platform I'm confident will stand the test of time.

And that is email marketing.

Email marketing has been around since 1978 and I don't see that changing. It's a marketing platform built around the core platform every country and generation uses for their communication, so I don't see it going away any time soon.

Why you should use email marketing

I'm not one for 'shoulds', but I'm okay saying that email is one platform you should have as part of your marketing strategy. Why? Because it will bring two key things to your growth:

1: Longevity and sustainability

As already mentioned, email is a platform we can trust will stick around for a long while, unlike others we use. We've seen how algorithm updates can damage your reach overnight: I've seen friends and clients lose their accounts only to have to start again from scratch, and we've all seen platforms come and go. While I'm a big fan of social media, I have to admit that it is a volatile platform for growth. But email isn't.

Email is not only a platform unlikely to experience many changes over the years, but also a platform where you have complete ownership over your community. You own your email list. Nobody has the power to take that away from you. If the worst were to happen and all other platforms disappeared, you'd still have a way to reach your community.

I meet so many business owners who are over-reliant on social media and as a result feel unstable and scared. That's where email can come in. It partners beautifully with social media to allow us to gather our most engaged people and breathe longevity into our marketing. If, like me, you want your online presence to still exist in five-plus years, email is your tool.

2: Conversion and sales

'We need to make more sales' and 'we have the people there but they aren't buying' are two things I hear from people a lot. A little digging often identifies a key reason why: they're not utilizing email.

Email marketing is a remarkable tool for nurturing community towards a sale. When done intentionally and consistently, your email list can become the most profitable part of your strategy. According to a study done by Mckinsey & Company,* email marketing is up to forty times more effective than social media. The same study showed that the purchasing rate is three times faster, too.

Why is it such an effective place to generate sales?

SALES ON SOCIAL

- Limited to one link, usually not directly on the content
- Speak to your whole community, no direction
- Little to no stats on how sales content performs
- Algorithms mean you have no control over who sees what, or if they see it at all
- Fit your sales pitch into a predetermined structure

SALES VIA EMAIL

- As many links as you want, however you want
- Speak directly to who you know is relevant, via segmenting and waitlists
- Clear metrics and scope for testing, can track behaviour to personalize follow-up content
- Complete autonomy over what is sent and when
- Say as much as you want, show as much as you want

*Source: www.mckinsey.com/capabilities/growth-marketing-and-sales/our-insights/why-marketers-should-keep-sending-you-emails

It's not that you *can't* sell via social media; it's more that email often gives you a more controlled, measurable and effective way of selling. I find a lot of the business owners I meet who feel uncomfortable around sales also enjoy introducing email as it allows for a more private and intentional invitation to buy.

We've been seeing email marketing wrong

If you feel an aversion to email marketing or can't quite picture how it would make sense for your business, I'm going to assume that's because you're not seeing it in the right way.

The email marketing we've seen from big companies has taught us that email = spam, that it's just a company's way of bombarding you with sales pitch after sales pitch, that it feels impersonal and irritating and that we only join by accident or because we want a discount code.

That is not the kind of email marketing I'm talking about here. I want us to see email as another platform where we serve, connect and nurture our community. If marketing is a conversation, email is just another platform we can use to start that conversation.

You likely think of your social media as a space to share value, and I want you to approach email with the same intention. It's content, not promotion.

Two types of emails to send

The phrase 'serve before you sell' is most true when it comes to email marketing. It's a space where you nurture in order to convert, so we can take from that the two core types of emails we can send:

Serve emails + Sell emails

> **TIP**
> When starting with email, pick a period of time to commit to sending 'serve' emails before trying to sell or being tempted to give up. I did three months of serve emails when I first began growing my list.

Let's look at each type in more detail:

SERVE EMAILS

What is the goal?
Deliver value to your list
(inform, inspire, entertain, relate);
this will deepen their connection
with you and increase their
understanding of your mission.

**What is the content
of the email?**
A clear and valuable
concept that is repeated
each time, gentle calls to
buy or take action.

How often do you send it?
Consistently – a minimum
of once per month.

Which metrics do we measure?
Open, replies.

SELL EMAILS

What is the goal?
Invite your list to take action
and buy / enquire / book, etc.

**What is the content
of the email?**
Key information about the
product or service, clear and
central calls to action or links.

How often do you send it?
TBD, whenever you are
launching or promoting
something.

Which metrics do we measure?
Click-throughs, conversions.

Revisiting the fish in a pond analogy we discussed earlier in the book, you could see it that your serve emails are about feeding those fish (keeping them in the pond, building their trust with you, giving them a taster of what you do) and the sell emails are when you're popping in your net and inviting them to take action.

You have to serve in order to sell. If you're yet to begin your email marketing or have been inconsistent so far, nail your serve emails, send them regularly and begin to grow your list, before you begin selling.

Creating a killer serve email concept

The goal is not for people to join your email list; the goal is for them to stick around. And the key to them sticking around is in the concept for your serve emails.

A list that is engaged, relevant and ready to buy is not created by chance, it is nurtured through valuable and consistent emails. So the first step to effective email marketing is nailing your email concept.

That is, what are you going to send your list?

At this point, I think we need to hold a brief funeral for the newsletter. You know the kind, where there's a pop-up on someone's website that says: 'Want to receive updates about company news? Join our newsletter!' And you think to yourself, 'Wow, I don't even keep up with the real news, let alone this random company's updates.'

Nobody wants a newsletter. They want valuable content. And that is what your concept should be.

The best email concepts are:

Valuable

Your email concept should contain clear value, whether it be sharing something informative, something inspiring, a relatable conversation or perhaps just a bit of entertainment. Question what that could look like to your community. What would they like to receive from you? If you could write them a letter you think they'd find interesting, what might you share?

Simple

Simplicity is key with email, for two main reasons:

1. To make it easy for you to talk about and promote your emails. If you can't sum up the benefit in someone joining your list, they won't take that step.
2. To make it easy for you to create. Email marketing can be a slow burner, so consistency is key. The simpler your emails are, the easier you'll find it to create them on a regular basis.

Personal

A person's inbox is an intimate space, so what if we allowed our emails to feel a similar way? Your subscribers don't want to hear a broadcast message for the masses; they want to feel like you're speaking to them, and the privacy of emails gives us permission to be that bit more personal. Could it be a way you bring people behind the scenes? Or perhaps share more insights from your own experience?

Named

As we're now grieving the loss of the newsletter, we need a new title for these emails! You don't have to take this step, but if you come up with a name for your emails, you'll find it much easier to promote them in a clear way and build people's understanding of them. For example, my weekly emails are called 'TheMidweek'. This allows me to use phrases like 'subscribe to TheMidweek to receive...' and 'This week on TheMidweek I shared...' when promoting my emails on other platforms.

How to grow your email marketing list

Once your emails have a concept, it's time to think about growing your list so people can receive the brilliance you're writing.

1 Talk about it!

People can't subscribe if they don't know about it, so ensure it's something you regularly speak about. Have sign-up forms across your website, promote it in your other content and use the valuable concept you've defined to get people to join.

2 Link it with other content

An easy way to ensure you talk about your emails on your other platforms is to create content that links with it. For example, on social media, you could document yourself writing the email and ask people for their insights. Or on your blog or podcast you could have a conversation that is a follow-up on the email you sent.

The only 'secret' to email success

is sending
something
people actually
want to open.

3 Make it your inner community

Your email list should be filled with your most engaged community and should also sit at the centre of your business, so treat it that way! Use it as the first platform to share news or updates, give those on your email list first access to discounts or rewards, and make those on your list feel appreciated. It will keep people there and make others want to join in.

4 Use free lead magnets

A lead magnet is where you offer something of value in exchange for people joining your list such as a PDF download, workshop or resource. I'm not against this strategy – it can be a great way to grow your list – but I think it needs to be done carefully. If this is the primary way people join your list, what you may notice is a high number on the list but a low number of subscribers actually engaging (opening, clicking, etc.). As we know, the value isn't in someone joining your list; it's in them sticking around. If you are going to use lead magnets, make it clear what people are signing up for and be okay with the fact that you may see a lower engagement rate from these subscribers.

How to sell to your email marketing list

Once you're serving your email list, you can begin to think about selling to them and encouraging conversion. Here are the three main ways you can do that:

Via your regular emails

Although the primary purpose of your regular emails is to serve, you can still create opportunities for your list to take action. An easy way to do this is to add banners at the bottom of your email template that can be customized each time you send an email to highlight a particular offer or an upcoming launch. I also like adding a little Public Service Announcement to the start or bottom of an email to deliver a quick promotion before or after the main value.

Via one-off sales emails

Whether it's because you're launching something new, wanting to promote your next availability or have a promotion that's linked to something seasonal, one-off sales emails are how you can deliver a focused call to action to your list. Be careful not to send these emails out too regularly, and when you do, keep them focused and clear.

Via targeted sales emails

Instead of sending sales emails to the whole of your list, one of the best ways to increase conversion without worrying that you're spamming everyone is to target your emails to specific subscribers. You could do this by sending it to a particular segment based on their behaviour (for example, your most loyal customers) or by getting people to opt into the waitlist (for example, sign up to be the first to know about X launching soon). By speaking to a smaller but more relevant list you'll be able to send more sales emails without worrying that you're irritating the rest of your list.

Regardless of which sales strategy you're using, the biggest key to an email that converts is in the messaging. Email is a primarily copy-based platform, so what you say is key. When selling, remember what we discussed earlier: people buy impact, not format. When you're selling something, get clear on why this is valuable for your community and bring that into your messaging as much as you can.

Email marketing tips

I could happily write about email for the rest of this book, but we have other topics to discuss! So let's round off with some quick tips you may find valuable:

Automate a welcome email

Write an email that introduces new subscribers to you, sets an expectation for what they are going to receive and gives them some immediate next steps or links to other content or platforms.

Make it personal

Ask people for their first name when they subscribe so you can personalize the 'to' field in your emails. It's a sure-fire way to increase their engagement.

Pick your subject line carefully

The job of your subject line is to entice people into opening it, so ensure it grabs attention and piques curiosity.

Check on mobile

We often write emails on desktop despite the fact that they're increasingly opened on phones, so do a test email and ensure the formatting and design also works on phones.

Cleanse your list

Removing inactive subscribers every six to twelve months will ensure your open rate stays healthy and you're only sending emails to those who are interested and relevant.

I spoke with Dee Dunne, Senior Director of Lifecycle Marketing at Intuit Mailchimp, the leading automation and email marketing platform, to understand what it takes to succeed:

'Email is a quality game, not a volume game. If your emails are landing in your audience's spam folders, focus on building out a quality subscriber list with engaged audience members and creating content they want to read. Optimizing email for good deliverability is about knowing your audience and building campaigns that keep them engaged.'

TIP
Keep the promotion clear and brief! In other words: get to the point.

Summary / Action

Key learnings:

1. Email marketing will stand the test of time.
2. Email marketing can provide better conversion than social media.
3. The traditional way of approaching email marketing is out.
4. Email is a space to serve before we sell.
5. Outlining a valuable, simple and personal email concept is the first step.
6. There are a number of ways we can sell via email; utilizing a mix of all of them is the best approach.
7. Clear messaging is key to email marketing conversion.

Action steps:

- If you're new to email marketing, outline your concept and come up with a one- or two-sentence description of it.
- If you're established via email, consider what action you could take to grow your list more intentionally.

CASE STUDY

Isobel Perl of PERL Cosmetics

I spoke to Isobel Perl, the founder of PERL Cosmetics, about the impact that email marketing has on her business.

Despite often going viral on social media, why is email marketing important to you?

Email marketing is incredibly valuable for us at PERL because you don't own the customer/follower data from social platforms. If we relied solely on social to generate sales, we'd be hoping that every video we post lands in front of a potential customer, which we all know doesn't happen. Growing our email marketing subscribers means we can talk directly to potential customers, offer them exclusive discounts and treat them like our V.I.PERLs.

What impact does your email marketing have on the business?

A growing email list means we can cover all bases when we run new offers, allowing us to communicate with customers across multiple platforms. It also means we can automate a lot of our flows, so as soon as someone signs up, they automatically go through a flow that is already set up and we don't need to lift a finger. Our automations bring in a lot of monthly store revenue too, with 70% of our email marketing revenue attributed to flows and 44% of our store revenue attributed to email marketing.

Any top tips for brands looking to utilize email?

Ensure you have a pop-up on your website to capture users as they land and have an enticing offer to encourage sign-ups.

Automations are your best friend, so make sure you have at minimum a welcome series and an abandoned checkout series.

Utilize personalization. This could be something as simple as having two thank you emails, one for a new customer and one for returning customers, through to something as detailed as person X likes vanilla, so let's upsell them similar flavours, whereas person Y likes fruity flavours so let's upsell them complementary flavours.

'44% of our revenue comes from email'

Top: By offering a first-order discount, Isobel encourages new customers to join her newsletter and make their first purchase. Her welcome email introduces people to the brand alongside giving them the code to use.

Bottom: Founder Isobel Perl and the products she sells through PERL Cosmetics.

PERL

NEW IN   SKINCARE   ACCESSORIES

Hey

THANKS FOR

SIGNING UP

Hey, thanks for signing up

Get 10% off your first order

GET 10% OFF YOUR FIRST ORDER

SIGN UP TO KEEP UP TO DATE WITH THE TEAM AT PERL HQ

What's your email?

What's your name?

Let us know when your birthday is for surprise...

SIGN UP

BY SIGNING UP, YOU ARE AGREEING TO RECEIVE EMAIL MARKETING

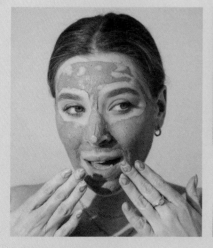

Psychotherapist Elsie Owen

Here's what service-based business owner and psychotherapist Elsie Owen has to say about using email marketing for a service.

You have an engaged social following, so why is email marketing important to you too?

There's a difference between people following my Instagram and people taking that extra step to sign up and be part of my email community. There's an extra level of connection; it somehow feels like there is less distance between us. When someone gives you a space in their inbox, it's a big deal – it means they are opting into hearing from you. I've noticed what a huge difference that makes both to how comfortable I feel about selling to them and the likelihood of them buying.

How do you ensure your emails are valuable to them?

I experiment with ideas and I invite feedback. I pay attention to open rates and any other data I can gather about how something is landing with people. I try to be responsive to what I'm learning about the people I'm wanting to reach, how they behave, what they find most meaningful and valuable, and why.

What impact have these emails had on your business and sales?

The majority of my sales come from email. People express a direct interest in my work, they get value from the non-salesy content I share with them, we start to build a relationship of sorts, and not only do I feel more comfortable selling to them because of this, but also they start to trust me enough to invest in what I'm offering.

There's something lovely about knowing that those on my email list have actively expressed their interest in hearing from me; there's a level of consent there that I really value. I enjoy the closeness that email offers. I feel more comfortable not just to advertise my offerings but to share more personally, and therefore connect more personally, with the people I might work with one day. Email is more private, it's more intimate and that really, really suits me, the work I do and the person I am.

Any top tips for people looking to utilize email?

Start somewhere – a monthly email will do more for you than no email at all. Be willing to experiment and not be very good at the start. Learn, find out, experiment and take advice from those with more experience than you.

Find a way not to take unsubscribes personally. Someone unsubscribing from your emails is unlikely to have anything to do with you, your worth or the value of what you're offering. It will probably be far more to do with who they are and what feels valuable to them in this season of their life. Instead of focusing on the few people who choose to unsubscribe from your emails, look instead at all the people who choose to stick with you; they are the people you should give your energy to.

ELSIE OWEN
@the_peoplepleasing_therapist

One of my friends is the most direct and pragmatic person I know. And she is the least people-please-y person I know, too.

I was at her house for dinner the other week and as we were chatting on her sofa after eating, she said, 'I'll need to go to bed soon.'

Something struck me about how easy she seemed to find it to name her need and essentially make it clear that she was ready for me to leave. I was inspired!

There was a clear and factual nature to what she was saying. An absence of discomfort or awkwardness and just a very simple truth: it was late, she was ready for bed, ready for me to leave.

Oh I loved every word of this

I adore your emails Elsie thank you!

Top: Emails don't need to be complicated or overly designed in order to be effective. The start of Elsie's email is both engaging and easy to follow – two things to aim for at the start of your email content.

Bottom: Positive replies from subscribers are good indicators that you're sending effective emails. People's inboxes are busy, so feedback like this is a great sign as it proves people are opening, reading and finding value in your content.

12.
Getting people to find you

TIP
Ask previous clients or customers how and where they first found you. This information is invaluable as it tells you what is and isn't working from your visibility efforts.

How do people discover your business? If that's a question you've been asking, then this is the chapter for you: here we'll look at the various exposure points available to you. This final group of 'platforms' is a collection of touch-points and tools that can drive visibility to your business.

Think of them like your top of funnel activity, or the actions that get fish into your pond in the first place. We will look specifically at four key ways to generate exposure:

1. Press and features
2. Paid ads
3. Collaborations
4. Creative marketing

(In the next chapter we will look at word of mouth and networking.)

Put yourself in the driver's seat

It can be tempting in business to sit back and wait for people to find us. If you can be lazy, I say go for it – but most of the businesses I meet don't want to be lazy. They want to take control of their visibility. They want to take action towards achieving their marketing goals.

So, although you can sit back and wait for others to offer you exposure, this chapter is for you if you're ready to take control.

I'll never claim to be an expert in every area under the wide umbrella of marketing strategy, so I ask industry experts for their insights and tips on how we can take control of our visibility and utilize these exposure points.

Press and features

Being featured in newspapers, magazines and publications will increase your visibility to new audiences and add credibility for your current community. Rosie Davies-Smith, the founder of PR Dispatch, an educational platform that helps e-commerce brands secure their own press coverage, generously shared her industry insights.

What is PR?

PR stands for public relations. It is the exercise of getting your brand or service mentioned in the press, or by a credible third party, but not paying for it. It builds credibility, trust, awareness, increases touch-points with your current audiences, and increases the visibility of not only your product or your service, but also your story, and you as the founder. PR is a crucial part of your marketing mix.

When is your business ready to pitch to the press?

Your business is ready to pitch to the press from day one. As soon as you have a presence, whether it be a website or a social media account, you are ready to get going.

One key thing you'll want to think about before pitching is your imagery. Strong pictures are key to securing quality press coverage so:

- If you're a service-based business and putting the founder at the forefront, get some photos of you and what you do. For example, a consultant may want images of them sitting round a table with clients or smiling from behind a laptop.
- If you're a product-based business, get some really sharp, strong images of your products with a clean background.

How do you pick the story or angle you want to pitch?

This varies, based on what's going on in your business and in the world at that time. So there's typically a mix of:

Topical

Link your story or expertise to something going on in the world. For example, if shops are closing down because of the economic crisis, and you've had to close two of your stores but your online business is booming, that's a story you should pitch at that point.

Regular features

A good example is Style List in *Stylist* magazine, which shares an article every week that features thirty products and will be looking for brands that are relevant for that time of year. Remember, they're compiling anywhere between five months and a few weeks ahead, depending on how often the publication is published.

Profile press

This is where an article shares an interview with the founder or tells their business story; they will be looking for a certain angle. Some may always focus on a mental health aspect, or a parenting publication may always focus on how people juggle family and business. Look for the common theme and then choose something from your story that matches up with that.

Tips for reaching out to journalists

Contact the right person

It's really important when you're pitching that you contact a person directly. Don't send the same email to everyone at the magazine; you want to contact the person who compiles that feature. Press move around all the time, so be sure to access a press database (for example, in PR Dispatch) to find the relevant contacts.

Write a concise email

They do not need your whole brand story, they need the nuggets that are relevant to them and their publication. If you're a visual business, attaching imagery as a low-resolution file will help support your pitches.

Send a follow-up email

Once you've pitched, stay on their radar: send another email or connect with them on LinkedIn. You might not be relevant at that moment, but it doesn't mean you won't be relevant in the future.

TIP

'You'll save yourself time pitching and following up if you're selective with who you pitch to. Do your research and consider what sort of content the journalist usually publishes, what they've already covered and what will actually align with the brand. Journalists want original content, so save yourself time pitching ideas to everyone and just tailor something to one person. They're much more likely to go for it.'
Ali Ball, health and fitness journalist

Paid ads

Paying to strategically reach new audiences and retarget those already connected to you can be a scalable way of growing. Nobody wants to waste their money by doing it wrong, so I spoke with Facebook Ads specialist Nieve Taylor to learn how we can utilize paid ads.

What are the best ways to use paid ads in a business?
Paid ads are often mistaken for only being good for e-commerce businesses, but that's not the case.

They can seriously accelerate your growth, customer base and reach by using targeting features like location, age, behaviours and interests online. Alongside using ads to convert, what's often overlooked and massively underrated is using them to increase your visibility and get new people into your buyer's journey, on autopilot.

One of the best strategies I see and use is to combine paid ads with email marketing and leverage your lead magnet to take cold audiences on an experience with your brand.

When is a marketing strategy ready for paid ads?
You're ready to starting using paid ads when:

You have a proven offer
Making at least ten organic sales of your product or service will validate that you have an offer people want, desire and need before you invest in ads. If people weren't buying it before, paying to get it front of more people won't necessarily sell your offer.

When you have the monthly budget
Ad results can take time to show, depending on the business and length of their buyer's journey, so it's important to consider what you can afford to invest IF you didn't get that return back.

It's also important to ensure you have the other parts of your marketing ready. Introducing paid ads will put you in front of your target market, but that will only be effective if your messaging is clear and your offer is positioned well.

Top tips for impactful ads

Refine the messaging in your copy.
There is so much competition out there that finding new and fresh ways to call out your customers' pain points and desires is more important than ever.

Demonstrate how your offer works, looks and benefits the customer.
Short and snappy videos of demos with voiceovers are leading the way right now.

Keep the creatives fresh.
Ad fatigue is not only bad for the performance of your ads, but can actually affect your reputation and put people off your business. Don't let the same ads run for a long time with no change.

Never stop testing.
You're never done; paid ads are always changing and evolving, so always continue to test.

Collaborations

Collaborating with other brands or individuals who align with your business can be a strategic (and fun!) way to be exposed to new audiences. When you're partnering with another business, you're basically creating an opportunity for their community to meet you and vice versa. Whatever your idea may be, here's how I'd suggest you go about it:

- Pick the right partner. Ensure whoever you're partnering with is aligned with your values, complements your mission and will have a relevant audience for you.
- Make it an easy yes. When pitching a collaboration idea, be really clear about what you're suggesting and how you want the other party to get involved.
- Be persistent. Putting yourself out there can be scary, but you've got to keep going until you get a response.

I love the way Kira Matthews, a mindset and manifestation coach, puts it:

'Your brain will assume that a no response is a rejection and you may start imagining "what if they see my email and think I'm a loser; what if they tell me they think I'm a loser? What if they tell everyone that I'm a loser and the word spreads like wildfire and ruins my whole business." Terrified at the prospect of our worst-case scenario coming true, most people stop. They don't send the email, and if they've sent the email once with no response, they don't dare send a follow-up.

But when we take a moment to ground our feet in reality, it is rarely the case that Julie from the dream brand you want to work with has seen your email or message and set fire to it. It's more likely that Julie is busy with a life of her own. It could even be possible that Julie has seen your email and begun mulling the idea over in her head. But you'll never discover that if you give up.

The rule I live by is to either get a yes or a no from the person you're wanting to connect with. No answer isn't a response.'

Creative marketing

Last but not least, we can get creative with the way we reach people! Whether it's getting out on the streets with some guerrilla marketing or giving away branded air fresheners, there are many ways you can create touch-points with your audience.

Here's how marketing expert Cloe Wadsworth did it:

'By stepping away from social media and getting creative with your marketing, you can reach a totally new audience. In one of my businesses we gave our community car fresheners as a freebie. We added "last tech on board", added our logo and branding, and within a week we had tripled our sales from the previous nine weeks, had over 300 people sign up to our mailing list and gained almost 1,000 followers... why? Because nobody in the industry had done it before, it was new, it was exciting and it was creative marketing at its finest! Social media is great, but it's also unpredictable. Get creative with marketing and think outside of the box.'

Lo Constantinou of Good Copy

Lo Constantinou founded and runs Good Copy, a bespoke CV, cover letter and LinkedIn writing business and employability specialist. In 2022 she was featured in Forbes by journalist Bianca Barratt. What happened next proves just how powerful press can be.

Where was your business before you got the feature?

Prior to the *Forbes* piece, I had been self-employed for around six months. I was actually in what I perceived to be a busy and positive place with the business prior to *Forbes,* also working as a copywriter in a freelance capacity for a small e-commerce brand.

I expected the piece to be a great content vehicle for me, legitimize me as a small business founder and give me some media credibility in my field. What I didn't expect was the incredible response.

What impact did the piece have on you and your business?

Wow, I don't even know where to begin.

To date, the piece has been read on the *Forbes* website 110,000 times, and been shared across all *Forbes*'s main social media platforms more than ten times. It has been shared by Anna 'Mother Pukka' Whitehouse, Kaytee 'The Nurse Mum' Jones and across dozens of parenting apps, websites and social media pages.

1. Sales: From the second the *Forbes* piece landed in February 2022, I've not needed to advertise my work or services. I've been booked up months in advance since early 2022, with my credibility skyrocketing and my work supporting hundreds of people as they navigate declined flexibility, career changes, discrimination, sexism at work, homelessness and more.

2. Opportunities: The piece has opened the door for conversations on female employment, the gender pay gap and the motherhood penalty, and has been a vehicle for me to secure features in national magazines, digital publications and upcoming speaking engagements.

3. Visibility: The piece has allowed me to reach a much wider demographic of potential clients, with my following on social media growing by around 9K in the last twelve months (with zero paid advertising).

Any tips for businesses considering PR as part of their strategy?

I was introduced to Bianca, the journalist, through someone in my network, so this is a great example of how your own connections can support you and positively impact you professionally! Don't underestimate the power of good old word of mouth.

Opposite: Being featured allowed Lo to use the claim across her website and marketing activity, giving people an immediate sense of trust in her work. It's also been seen by 100,000+ people and driven a huge amount of traffic to her platform.
Below: Lo's feature in *Forbes* catapulted her and her business to new heights of success. A dedicated article like this one is something many entrepreneurs dream of.

Forbes

FORBES > LEADERSHIP > FORBESWOMEN

This Woman Writes Killer Resumes For Mothers Returning To Work. Here's What She Wants You To Know.

Bianca Barratt Senior Contributor ⓘ
I write about women in business and issues surrounding women at work.

Follow

Feb 11, 2022, 12:12pm EST

'One press feature in *Forbes*, and I've been booked up for the last eighteen months and counting.'

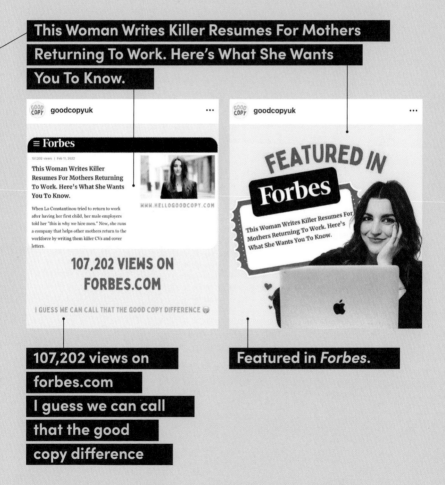

This Woman Writes Killer Resumes For Mothers Returning To Work. Here's What She Wants You To Know.

107,202 views on

forbes.com

I guess we can call

that the good

copy difference

Featured in *Forbes*.

Summary / Action

Key learnings:

1. Visibility can come from a number of different sources – press, paid ads, collaborations and networking.
2. You don't have to be everywhere to be visible; you can intentionally choose which approach will suit you and your goals best.
3. You're ready to pitch to the press from day one of your business.
4. Paid ads are best used once you've got proof of concept and have the budget to comfortably experiment and take risks.
5. Growing your network is important, but it's just as important to nurture the relationships you already have.
6. It's normal to feel scared when putting yourself out there, so expect rejection and be persistent when reaching out or pitching.

Action steps:

- Ask your clients and customers how and where they found you (consider adding this question to your checkout process or feedback form).
- Outline the ways you want to drive visibility for your business.
- Map out your weekly or monthly action steps to fulfil your chosen method of visibility.

13.
Networking and word of mouth marketing

The best marketing in the world is marketing that you don't have to do. Sound too good to be true? It's not, and it goes by the name of word of mouth.

Alice Benham Dictionary
Word of mouth: past clients and customers or those in your industry spreading the word about your business on your behalf.

Word of mouth is incredibly powerful, and something we all want more of, right?

I mean, why wouldn't we? Word of mouth marketing means: others are doing the work on our behalf.

Them endorsing our work means the person they share with is more likely to trust us.

It proves that we are succeeding at nurturing a community and delivering a great product or service.

In an ideal world, our buyer's journey doesn't end at the decision stage; it continues with those people becoming avid referrers of what we do. Or 'brand fans', as some marketing experts call them.

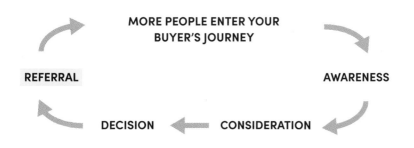

MORE PEOPLE ENTER YOUR
BUYER'S JOURNEY

REFERRAL

AWARENESS

DECISION

CONSIDERATION

How to encourage your clients or customers to refer you

Referrals are gold dust in business, but they can often feel out of our control. Part of what makes them so effective is how organic and authentic they are, so while we don't want to try and engineer them, we can think about how to encourage them.

Here's what I've learned helps generate more word of mouth marketing:

1 Optimize your client/customer experience

On top of just being brilliant at what you do or sell, delivering it with excellence is a key step to making people rave about you. It's all in the details. Whether it be your customer service or client onboarding, look at all of your touch-points and consider how they could be up-levelled to give your customers and clients a reason to shout about you.

2 Provide opportunities to share

Ever wondered why brands make such a big deal of their packaging? Or why service providers might send their clients a welcome gift in the post? Or why a landing page after you purchase might have a fun meme or graphic on it? It's to give you something easy to share. Someone randomly telling their own audience about your business may feel a little out of place, but if you give them something to share or focus the recommendation around, I bet you'll see an increase in notifications saying 'X tagged you in their post'.

3 Ask for it and reward it

This is a simple tip but not one to ignore. Often people will happily share on your behalf; you just haven't planted the idea in their head yet. Make a point to mention how much it means when clients or customers refer you, and if you want to, reward it. We don't want the reward to encourage people to do it inauthentically, but when we affirm the correct behaviour, we're likely to get more of it. Whether you send a simple thank you message or offer a discount code or a freebie, some form of reward will encourage those who would have shared anyway to do even more of it.

This is what Abby Munro, founder and director of Paper & Word, does. Her company's book sleeves are shared by customers on a daily basis and as a result they sell out of their new stock each month.

'We make a point to reply to every comment and tag on social media, and regularly reshare our favourites. We find this only increases the volume of shares (and sales!), as customers want a share of the limelight themselves.'

The other way we can look at this is through our community and network doing the marketing for us.

Growing your network

Your network is simply your group of connections who know about you and your business. Typically, a network consists of those in the same industry as you and other professionals whose work is in some way relevant to yours.

Taking action to grow your network won't necessarily have a direct and measurable impact on your sales, but will absolutely pay off in the long run. The phrases 'it's not what you know, it's who you know' and 'your network is your net worth' are ones I find a little frustrating. Does that mean we're creating an environment where those without the privileged access to networks struggle to succeed? However, there's no denying that your network is valuable, and I can say that as someone who has experienced it first-hand.

Many of the clients who have come to me and the opportunities I've been offered have in some way been facilitated or helped by a member of my network. Whether it be a journalist, an event curator or an industry thought leader, much of my growth has been thanks to this network I've created.

I do find the word 'network' a little icky, because what we're really talking about here is business friends. People. Relationship building.

Something that when done intentionally won't just help your marketing and growth but will provide invaluable support to you as an individual.

I want you to think about two things here:

1 How are you growing your network?

What actions are you taking to actively put yourself out there and meet new people? Are you attending events, joining memberships and making the first move to reach out to someone you admire?

The more we approach networking with authenticity and the sooner we start to treat people with kindness, the quicker we'll see the benefits come back to us.

2 How are you nurturing your network?

What are you doing to stay connected to those you've already met? Are you offering them opportunities too? Staying connected online? Treating them like an actual friend as opposed to someone to track on a spreadsheet?

While making connections is great, there is an important next step: nurturing them. Being known by lots of people is no use if a) they don't remember you long-term, and b) you don't deepen and strengthen those relationships.

Tips on nurturing your network

Here is advice from Stefanie Sword-Williams, founder and author of *F*ck Being Humble*, about how to nurture your connections:

If you want to build and sustain a network, my advice is simple: treat them like a friend. I don't mean drunk calling on a weekend or getting feedback on outfit checks, but adding value to them to showcase why they should create time for you. Sometimes we overthink things or we're so worried about looking needy we let amazing connections slip through the net. Here are some tried and tested examples to nurture new connections that have worked for me:

TIP
Look on event ticket websites like Eventbrite to find relevant networking opportunities in your area.

1 Share a useful resource. Instead of the standard 'just checking in' message, find a podcast, article, video or social media post you think would resonate with them, and send it over email with a message on why you think they'll like it.

2 Introduce them to someone. A great way to show a new connection you can add value to them without needing something in return is by introducing them to someone new. Show them this isn't a transactional relationship, and you're interested in supporting them too.

3 Send them something in the post. We all know emails are easy to forget and people are always drowning in them, so send them something physical to surprise them if you want to be memorable.

4 Invite them to something. If you're going to an event, grab an extra ticket and suggest you go together. It's a great a casual way to form a relationship with them that's not centred around work.

If I had to sum up how to mobilize your community, customers and network to market for you it would be this: be great at what you do and be really kind while you do it.

There's not much more to it than that. If you do good work and treat people well, they'll want to help you win, and you'll soon see your reputation going wider than your voice alone could ever take it.

Conclusion

Your platforms are the 'where' of your marketing strategy. They are the component you'll want to come back to any time you're considering adding something new into the mix or simply feeling like you need an injection of intention.

Now let's look at the second half of our plan, which is all about content...

Summary / Action

Key learnings:

1. If you can utilize word of mouth, your marketing will be done on your behalf.
2. While we can't control or force people to refer us, we can take action to encourage it.
3. Effective networking isn't just about meeting new people; it's also about nurturing relationships with those you're already connected to.

Action steps:

- Look at the ways you're encouraging word of mouth. Can you take any action to encourage this further?
- Outline your networking approach. How are you connecting with new and relevant people in your industry? Just as importantly, how are you nurturing those relationships?

Content: what are you doing?

Content is what makes or breaks a marketing strategy. If your platforms are the stage, your content is what you say when you're up there.

Let's look at all the ways we can up-level our content, from creating pillars and keeping it personal to harnessing video and increasing sales.

14.
Social media content

If your platforms are where you're showing up, your content is what you're showing up with. It's the contents of your conversation. Okay, that's a lot of Cs, but you get my gist.

The content we create is fundamental to the success we'll have online, on social media in particular. Your content is what connects people to you, spreads the word about your business, encourages conversion and nurtures conversation. It's the part of our marketing strategy that does the heavy lifting. So we want to think about it intentionally.

Content pillars

Content pillars. Content buckets. Content bowls... however you've heard them talked about, they exist to do the same thing: help us show up with ease.

It's not enough to just say 'cool, I'm showing up on LinkedIn, off I go...' We need to think intentionally about what we're going to be posting. Why? Because if not, a lovely concoction of fear, overwhelm and indecision will stop us from creating content.

So it's time we thought about content more intentionally, by defining your content pillars.

There are a number of different ways to approach content pillars. I want you to define yours through the lens of the buyer's journey. As a reminder, our content exists to do three things:

Expose > nurture > convert

So approaching our content pillars with theory in mind, there are four types of content pillars you'll want to use in order to effectively facilitate the buyer's journey.

1. Serve
2. Connect to you
3. Show what you do
4. Ask

By looking at your content in these four ways, you'll show up strategically and confidently. Let's look at them in more detail.

1 Serve

For those at the start of their buyer's journey or simply looking for value, this type of content will draw in new people and connect to those who are curious about your work. Serve content provides valuable and relevant content to your ideal audience.

Value can come in different forms – informing, inspiring, entertaining, relating, educating – so it's important to consider what value will look like to your potential clients and customers.

Your serve content will build people's trust with your expertise, show them you are a voice in your industry and help them to start considering the problem you solve or the desire you fulfil.

To understand your serve content, consider which topics you want to talk around that are relevant to what you do and who you're trying to reach. What do you want to be known for? This content should be positioning you as exactly that.

2 Connect to you

When people are at the second stage of the buyer's journey, consideration, they're asking two things: do I want your thing, and do I want it from you?

This content pillar is about answering that second question by connecting people to who we are as businesses or business owners. Back in Chapter 4 we discussed our purpose and values (that is, why people choose us); this is the time for that work to shine. It's all well and good us knowing why we're great, but now we've got to communicate it!

Whether it's bringing people behind the scenes, sharing your story, demonstrating your values or simply sharing something personal, this content is all about connecting people to you.

People buy from people. And your biggest USP against competitors is you. So how about we brought some of that into your content?

3 Show what you do

As I said above, the two questions people are asking in the consideration phase of the buyer's journey is: do I want your thing, and do I want it from you? Well, this content pillar will help them answer the first part of the question.

Very important reminder: if people don't know what you do, they won't be able to buy it.

Sounds obvious, right? But it's something I think we all need to hear.

There's a concept called 'knowledge bias', which is where we assume others have the same context and understanding that we do. It shows up a lot in marketing and has a particularly detrimental effect by stopping us from telling people what we do.

We think they already know. We assume they get it. And we decide it was enough to tell them that one time six months ago.

No.

You need to be clear and repetitive in showing people what you sell, who it's for, how it works, and why they should buy it. Because if they don't know they can't buy.

The restaurant analogy

Let me give you an analogy that will show you how silly it is for us to never do this content. It's like you've started a restaurant but there are no menus and no waiters, meaning potential customers are sitting there unsure a) what they can buy and b) how to buy it. They're left there to either walk away and find a clearer restaurant or find their way into the kitchen, peer at what the chefs are making and ask for some themselves.

That would be a ludicrous way to run a restaurant, so why do we do the same with our content?

We give away loads of free value, build connections and then leave people totally unaware of what we sell, hoping they'll figure it out on their own?

Let's stop doing that and ensure our audiences know what we sell. How? By showing it.

The thought of repetitively telling people what we sell sounds boring because it is. But showing people what we sell – now, that's an interesting way of being repetitive.

Product-based:

Want to show your product? Show the journey of making it.

Want to show what's included in an order? Show the packing process.

Want to show the impact your product will have? Show a lifestyle image or customer photo of it being used.

Service-based:

Want to show what you do? Show your day and the client work you're doing.

Want to show the care and work you put into your service? Show people behind the scenes by documenting your client process.

Want to show who you work with? Show a past client's transformation by celebrating their win.

By showing, not telling, we're able to be repetitive about what we do without it becoming irritating.

So the key prompts for you to consider are:

- What do I want people to know about my offering?
- What are their FAQs that I could answer in my content?
- How can I show rather than tell?

4 Ask for the sale

So we've given value, connected people to us and shown what we do. The final type of content that seals the deal and encourages conversion is asking for the sale.

Inviting people to take action is a simple way we can increase our sales without it feeling like we're throwing out a sales pitch. After all, if people don't know, they can't go!

Asking for the sale can be as simple as reminding people of your availability and letting them know when to enquire, mentioning the limited stock left and where to buy, or promoting a waitlist for a future launch.

It's something you'll most frequently do as a call to action at the end of other pieces of content, but it can also be a piece of content on its own.

So what is the next step you're encouraging people to take? And when are you asking for the sale?

Using your content pillars

Once you've defined your content pillars, the most important step is to use them.

My top tip is to see your content like a magazine.

Sometimes we can put far too much pressure on individual pieces of content, when in actual fact it's a team effort. The simplest way to think of it is like a magazine, where there's a valuable article on one page, followed by an ad on another, followed by a personal story on another. If everything was just valuable articles they'd never encourage sales, whereas if everything was an ad they wouldn't keep people engaged.

The mix of content is what makes it effective. And your social media content is no different.

TIP

If you're showing up on social media for the first time, I'd suggest beginning by sharing pillars 1 and 2: serve and connect people to you. The more 'salesy'-feeling content of 3 and 4 is best shown to an already engaged community, so focus on building relationships and then begin inviting the sale.

TIP

Put a reminder in your schedule or an alarm on your phone that periodically reminds you to sell, especially if it's for an offering that's always available.

Summary / Action

Key learnings:

1. People can't buy your thing if they don't know what your thing is.
2. Content pillars are ways to categorize the key topics you cover in your content.
3. The right content pillars will make it easier to show up strategically and consistently.
4. The four key pillars you'll want, in order to be facilitating the buyer's journey, are: serve, connect to you, show what you do, ask.
5. Every piece of content will work together to achieve the end goal, like a magazine.

Action steps:

- Define your content pillars, using the four types as a starting point.
- Explore content ideas for each pillar, giving yourself the space you need to spark new ideas.

Each piece of content is like a puzzle piece,

working together to form a picture about who you are and what you do.

CASE STUDY

Sophie Miller of Pretty Little Marketer

Sophie started building Pretty Little Marketer in 2020 and has since seen first-hand the power of great content. She's nurtured a community of 350,000-plus in three years, speaks at some of the biggest UK conferences, has a constant stream of sponsorships with brands including Adobe, YouTube and Meta, and is approached to work with some of the UK's biggest brands. I spoke with her to understand the secrets to her content success.

How do you create content that you know will connect with your community? How do you get your ideas?

Systemized ideation! Waiting for ideas to spring to mind just won't do it, not if you want an effective and reasonably stress-free process. You couldn't whip up a meal in an empty kitchen, right? Here's a few ways I do it:

Inspire yourself with an FAQ. I track all of my most asked questions, gathering them from places like my comment section, DMs or IG Story Q&As. Community groups are also a killer place for finding out what your audience want to know, and what they're struggling with right now.

Systemize your saves: bookmarking a blog post or saving that TikTok isn't enough. The saved folder is where ideas go to die. If by some miracle you do come back to it later, what are you going to do with it? Read it until something pops out? That's a time waster. Systemize it like this instead...

Every time you save a link, or see a post you want to come back to, don't just screenshot it for later. Save the link, and immediately note down three content ideas off the back of it. It's fresh in your mind, it gets your brain cogs moving and it means when you come back to it later, you're not left bamboozled and confused at why a random link is in your Notes section.

Organic growth can feel like you're shouting in the abyss, so how do you stand out from the crowd?

Flip 'how can I get more followers?' to 'how can I create content worth following?' What do audience members get when they follow you? Do they get easy and actionable tips? Do they get affordable fashion

alternatives? Do they get inspiration through your brand and founder story?

Everything you share needs to have purpose, and it must be an exchange. Before pressing the post button, pause and challenge yourself with a 'so what?' Our product makes your hair super shiny – great, so what? This is what I do in a day: fun! So what? What's the purpose? What does the viewer GET from that piece of content? The more you give, the more you get.

How can we create great content?
Be consistently great: If you ordered five takeaways per week, and only two were great, you'd 1. have to be mad rich, ha ha! But 2. You'd quickly be turned off because the reward isn't worth the sacrifice.

Give value: Make your content an exchange. Every post should leave your audience with something more than they had before they found you, whether it's a new tip or some inspiration or motivation.

Speak directly to your reader: The power of a 'you' or 'us' should not be underestimated.

Have FUN and get excited: I talk a lot on social media about how the host sets the tone. If the host is excited, the audience are excited. I mean, how fun would a concert with a bored, lacklustre Beyoncé be compared to a concert with a hyped and happy Beyoncé?

Previous page: While her community building primarily takes place online, Sophie hosts in-person events to bring the PLM community together for a more in-depth learning and networking experience. Events are a great way to make an online community feel more tangible and connected to you.

This page: By staying connected to her community, whether through sharing helpful resources or starting an interesting conversation, Sophie can create content that will be of clear value and relevance to them.

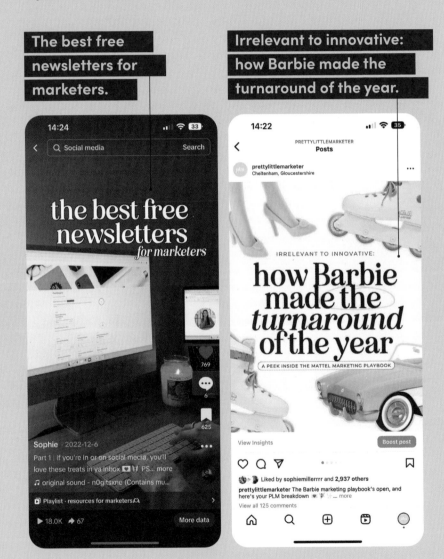

The best free newsletters for marketers.

Irrelevant to innovative: how Barbie made the turnaround of the year.

15.
People buy from people

Customers with an emotional relationship with a brand have a 306% higher lifetime value.* It won't cut it to just hide behind your product or service and let that do the talking; consumers want to connect with you. Either you as a business or you as an individual.

- Competition is rising.
- Consumers are getting pickier.
- Loyalty is harder than ever to create.

This tells us that people buy from people, so we need to care about our brand.

Alice Benham Dictionary
Brand: the unique qualities that appeal to your target audience and encourage them to choose you over a competitor: your story, personality, values and approach.

Put simply, your brand is why people choose you. When you build a personal brand through content, it speaks for you when you're not in the room. By humanizing your business and making content about more than just your product, four things will happen:

1 You'll stop competing on price

If all you share is your offering and there's a number of other businesses selling something similar, you're going to find yourself in the uncomfortable position of competing on price. Since that'll be the only real difference between you and the other options in front of them, you'll either have to cut margins or see a drop in sales.

Sharing more personal content will give you an edge: a reason for consumers to pick you above a competitor.

*Source: www.linkedin.com/pulse/loyalty-program-statistics-trends-surprise-delight-coniq/#:~:text=57%25%20of%20
consumers%20spend%20more,a%20306%25%20higher%20lifetime%20value

2 Customer loyalty and referrals will increase

Data shows that when customers feel connected to a brand, 57% will increase their spending and 76% will buy from them over a competitor.* This tells us that when a consumer has an emotional relationship with the brand they're buying from, they're more likely to come back again (hello, repeat sales) and also refer others (hello, free marketing). Selling to an old customer will always be more efficient and profitable than finding a new one, so give people a reason to remember and like your business.

3 Your reputation will stand the test of time

One of my favourite benefits to building a more personal brand is that it will bring sustainability to your marketing. Take my business as an example: if when I started out as a social media manager I only ever shared content about this and nothing else, I would have lost people's attention and interest when I pivoted to working as a marketing strategist. Businesses evolve and change, so connecting people to the heart of your business, which won't change, will keep your community connected regardless of what you're selling.

4 External opportunities will be open to you

If getting more press, being booked as a speaker or even going on someone's podcast is on your list of marketing goals, a more personal brand will open you up to these.

Bianca Barratt, journalist and founder of The Scoop, says: 'Having a strong personal brand makes you more appealing to the media because they know you already have some skill in telling captivating stories that connect with an audience. When you have a clear and consistent image, it shows that you're trustworthy and knowledgeable, making journalists and outlets eager to feature you in interviews, collaborations and news coverage because they're confident you're going to add value.'

On top of all those reasons, it can be fun to create more personal content. Sure, we all likely have some resistance around putting ourselves out there (more on that later), but there's something gratifying about feeling like you are reflected in what you share. That you don't just have a faceless, lifeless online presence.

How to humanize your business

Step 1 Define your brand

Before putting anything out there, we need to know what we're trying to say. What personality do you want your business to have? What areas of your behind the scenes does it make sense for you to share? Why do people choose your business?

The more connected you are to why people choose you, the easier you'll find it to bring this into your content. If you feel unclear on this, go back to Chapter 4, where we looked at defining your values.

Step 2 Show your brand

Now you know what you're trying to demonstrate, you can start bringing it into your content. There are many ways to do this, but they all link back to the same concept: bringing people behind the scenes. Let your community peek into the metaphorical factory of your business and in doing so connect them to who you are as a company.

Here are just a few ways to do that:

- Show the process of a product being made.
- Share your origin story.
- Empower your team to build their brands.
- Demonstrate your values.
- Celebrate your wins.
- Bring your personality into your content.

*Source: www.linkedin.com/pulse/loyalty-program-statistics-trends-surprise-delight-coniq/#:~:text=57%25%20of%20 consumers%20spend%20more,a%20306%25%20higher%20lifetime%20value

Implying your brand: visuals and voice

Alongside content that directly shows your brand, it's important to think about how the rest of your content can imply who you are as a business. This will be through your visuals and voice.

Your visuals can connect people to your brand by:

- Picking a visual identity (colours, fonts, graphics) that reflect your brand and using them consistently and cohesively across all channels. For example, I want my stationery brand, On Paper, to come across as simple, impactful and intentional, which is why I use a greyscale colour palette and very clean designs. A business wanting to come across as playful and engaging may go for something more colourful.
- Using people in your content to literally show that you're humans. One of the easiest ways to humanize your brand is to bring humans into your content... that is, you and your team. Whether it's by talking to the camera, using a voiceover or simply sharing clips and photos with people in them, you'll see a much higher engagement rate when you show up as a person. (More on this in the next chapter.)

Your tone of voice can operate in a similar way to your visuals by implying who you are as a brand.

Humanize your brand, but do it with boundaries

One of the biggest misconceptions around humanizing a brand is that we should share absolutely everything... because that's authentic, right? Take it from someone who has made this mistake the hard way: you don't have to, and you probably shouldn't share everything online.

TIP
Create a central 'brand' document that captures the visuals and tone of voice you want your business to use. This will make it easier for you and any team members to portray these elements consistently.

An authentic personal brand isn't about broadcasting every moment of your day and every hardship you experience. An authentic personal brand is about curating what feels relevant and comfortable to share.

Here's the sweet spot for personal content:

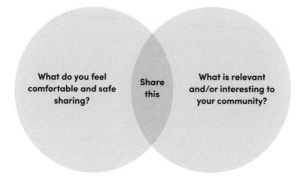

What is relevant to share?

Sharing the behind the scenes of your business isn't about telling people everything, and building a personal brand is not about becoming an influencer overnight. It's about sharing some content that you know will be relevant and interesting to your community.

You may share with your community a love for travel, so maybe it's relevant to document some of your trips. You may notice they enjoy when you talk more about the behind the scenes of the business, so maybe you start giving insights into what's happening day to day. Your business may revolve around fitness, so you document some of your own journey. They might love cats and you have a cat... so you share the cat.

Those small examples demonstrate how simple this content can be. We really don't need to share everything, but instead identify a couple of key topics that connect to people.

What feels comfortable to share?

Repeat after me: I'm allowed to have boundaries when building a personal brand; boundaries around both what I say and when I say it.

This is a lesson I learned the hard way. I used to think 'authenticity' meant sharing anything and everything. And I mean it. I would document family trips, announce on social media that I'd broken up with my boyfriend, and cry online about business challenges. It was a lot, and it was actually doing more damage than good.

The internet is an inherently nosy place, and it can be easy to fall into the trap of sharing more vulnerable content for the sake of engagement.

But that's dangerous for both you and your community. Not only because you deserve privacy and may not want people weighing in on vulnerable experiences, but also because your community deserves content that is created intentionally, not just spewed out like a one-sided therapy session.

Here are two things to think about:

1 What do you share?

We've talked already about identifying what content is relevant, so I want you to give yourself permission to not share some parts of your life or business. I personally don't share anything to do with my 'normal life' friends or family. I have clients who don't share their manufacturing process due to fear of competitors seeing. Whatever your reasons are, you're allowed to curate your online presence and leave some topics off the table. I promise you'll still come across as human.

2 When do you share?

The timing of personal content often determines if it's effective or damaging.

There's a quote I heard years ago that perfectly sums this advice up:
Share scars, not wounds.

Wounds are present experiences. They're fresh, sticky, painful to touch and not a fun experience for either side.

Scars are in the past. We can share them with hindsight, it doesn't feel uncomfortable for either side, and the topic has a conclusion.

If sharing your business challenges, wins or even personal experiences is important to you, I'd really encourage you to adopt this concept. It's less about what you share and more about when you share it. So next time you feel tempted to put out something intimate ask yourself: does this feel like a wound or a scar?

Humanizing your brand with confidence

Showing your face and bringing more personality into your content can come with a sense of fear. What if people think it's silly? What if I get trolled? What if that friend I haven't seen for fifteen years sees it? Worries like these can hold us back from showing up, so here are my top tips for building confidence:

Take baby steps

You build a muscle by using it, so start in an area or way that feels the easiest.

Look at the evidence

Your brain will come up with all the ways it could go wrong, but what evidence do you have that it's gone well in the past?

Block unhelpful eyes

If you're worried about the opinions of friends and family, mute them from your content to help you focus on who you really want to reach.

I asked cognitive behavioural psychotherapist Natalie McCandless how we can navigate fear when it crops up:

'We are social creatures, and fear of doing something different can bring out the critical voice and lead us into anxiety. This has come from our ancestors, when being outside of the group meant certain death. We can learn to override this.

Stop briefly. Take a moment to zoom out. Observe what is really going on. Write down the worrying thought. Is it really accurate? Pause. Take a breath. Practise self-compassion and kindness. What would you say to someone you love who was having these thoughts?

You can even thank the critical voice for showing up and trying to keep you safe! But be sure to let it know that it's not necessary or welcome here.'

Summary / Action

Key learnings:

1. Humanizing your brand will increase sales, customer loyalty and long-term growth.
2. Your brand is why people choose you – your personality, approach and values.
3. Creating behind-the-scenes content is the easiest way to show your brand.
4. You can also use your visuals and tone of voice to imply your brand.
5. Having boundaries around what you share and when you share it is a healthy approach.
6. You don't have to share everything to be authentic.
7. A lack of confidence will likely try to get in the way. Baby steps, blocking others and looking for the evidence will help.

Action steps:

- Reflect on what personal content you could share to connect your community to you and the behind the scenes of your business.
- Explore your own personal boundaries – what do and don't you feel comfortable sharing publicly?
- Create a piece of content that humanizes your business.

Rachel Harris of striveX®

Rachel Harris, co-founder and director of accountancy practice striveX®, has built the personal brand accountant_she® to grow their client base, increase revenue streams and build towards future opportunities.

striveX® is its own brand, so why did you make the decision to create accountant_she® as a personal brand alongside it?

When I started my personal brand accountant_she®, the accountancy practice striveX® already existed. I had done some market segmentation to understand how small business owners were behaving during the pandemic and I discovered that they were spending a lot of their time on social media. I wanted a brand that would become a pipeline of new work into the practice and act as my own personal brand, and I knew social media would respond better to a personal brand, rather than striveX® on its own.

What impact has your approach made?

My personal brand has helped us become one of the most rapidly scaling accountancy practices. In 2020, the business was a team of two with fifty clients, £5,000 of new work coming in each month and a 65% conversion rate. In 2023, we have eighteen full-time employees, 700-plus clients, £110,000 new work coming in each month and an 85% conversion rate!

The increase in sales and conversion is all down to building trust, because by the time someone books a call to become a client, they've usually already consumed a lot of our content. They've seen the team, they've consumed our educational content, they've consumed our pre-meeting resources and had lots of their questions answered already, so before they call they already know, like and trust our brand. I've had clients tell me afterwards that it literally didn't matter what price I quoted them, they'd already decided they wanted to work with us.

Alongside that we have an employee waiting list that helps us attract the industry's best talent, and my personal brand alone has become a six-figure business with ten income streams.

What are your top tips for using your personal brand to grow a business?

A personal brand is not about you. So many people get caught up in their heads about confidence, not being ready and what people will think of them. They think it's self-promotion, vanity, bragging and all about you. It's not like that at all. It's about two things:

1. Reputation and how people perceive you: It's the conversations people are having about you when you're not in the room. Building a personal brand is putting you back in the driver's seat; it gives you control over the reputational narrative that already exists for you. You can build a personal brand to drive and shape your own narrative, or you can let chance or an algorithm do it for you.

2. Impact: It's about maximizing the impact you can have on your audience and those around you. For me, accountant_she® has always been impact-driven. It's been about helping the most people, delivering financial education in free, accessible and consumable content, it's about lowering the barriers to entry surrounding finances and financial education. Building a personal brand has simply helped me to maximize that impact.

Case study: Rachel Harris **143**

Yonder

Wondering how you can mobilize your team to help humanize the company and build their own personal brands?

Yonder is a credit card for city adventurers that has a unique take on loyalty rewards, and is disrupting the market in more ways than one. Despite being in an industry filled with cold and faceless companies, Yonder actively encourages its team to build personal brands. By the sounds of it, it's working in their favour.

'As a platform used by lots of investors, founders and early adopters, LinkedIn has been powerful for us from the very start of Yonder's journey – it's been a place of support and guidance as the business started out, it connected us with more investors, and it continues to be a route to new customers and talent.

We also utilize the platform to boost exposure around our marketing efforts and, as a result, achieve press coverage. LinkedIn is a great opportunity for virality, but it can rarely happen without the team playing a role in promoting it.'

Here are their tips:

Encourage, don't enforce: We're an inherently social business, so sharing Yonder socially through our team network is always encouraged, but not enforced! We know not everyone feels comfortable putting themselves out there in the way that others do, so it's important for each team member to find their own approach.

Let the team take the stage: Our CEO doesn't take on all aspects of Yonder's external communication. Members from our Experiences, Engineering and Marketing teams are often podcast guests and conference speakers. Anyone who's keen to take on that sort of role is supported and given full autonomy over how they want to communicate with guidance where they need it, provided they feel comfortable with our Yonder principles and the reasons why we're building the business.

Top: By running events and inviting its team to host the evening, Yonder empowers employees to be visible and represent the brand. The 'Women and Money' series allowed customers to feel more connected to the company and introduced them to the people behind the business, increasing loyalty and trust.

Bottom: It's widely known that many angel investors look to back people, not businesses, so it's likely that Yonder's efforts to build personal brands online helped with raising £62.5 million in 2023.

Women and Money

Bridging the gap between women and finance

FREE event – Wednesday 23rd November From 6.30pm, 69 Old Street EC1V 9HX

HOST
Ellie Austin-Williams
Founder of This Girl Talks Money

PANELLISTS

Connie Osborne
Editorial Business Director at Hearst UK

Alice Benham
Business & Marketing Strategist for Value-Driven Entrepreneurs

Sophia Ufy Ukor
Founder & CEO at Violet Simon

→ THIS JUST IN → BIG NEWS → STOP SCROLLING →

SERIES A

£62.5 million

16.
Harnessing the power of video

Video content is on the rise. Recent studies shows that as many as 91% of consumers want to see more online video content from businesses.* I don't see that trend changing any time soon.

Social media platforms are increasingly promoting video-based features – and that isn't because they fancy it, it's because consumers want and enjoy video-based content. It's easy to consume, engaging and, when done right, is an incredible tool for communicating your message. Put simply: if you're not modernizing your content with video, you may get left behind.

The experts agree. Jess Wreford, Chief Creative Officer of Antler Social, believes video is the future of marketing: 'Video is the only fully human way we're able to show up. We can show people things within a matter of seconds that they wouldn't have been able to visualize without video.'

Long-form versus short-form videos

There are two primary types of videos you can create, and each has its own purpose.

Short-form video is great for capturing attention, communicating a brief message and leaving the viewer with one key takeaway (such as thirty- to ninety-second clips on social media).

Long-form video is best for communicating a more in-depth and detailed message, like telling a full story or delivering a number of insights at once (a YouTube video, a one-hour workshop).

A simplified summary would be that short form is for finding new audiences, whereas long-form will typically be for those already in your community. The type you use depends on your goals and what you want to communicate.

Ten video ideas for your business

1. Document a day in the life at your business.
2. Show the process of designing a new product.
3. Speak to camera, sharing one valuable tip.
4. Tell a story about a time when you learned a lesson.
5. Interview people about a topic your business is related to.
6. Put text over a B-roll clip to deliver an inspiring or informative insight.
7. Use trending audio or music to create an entertaining and relatable video.
8. Show the transformation your service provides.
9. Pack an order on video, showing your items and packaging.
10. Tour your office or work space.

I could easily continue that list, but the point I'm making is that if there's something you want to communicate, I'll bet there's a way you can use video to say it.

As well as being an engaging format, video is one of the easiest types of content to reuse and repurpose. All of the clips used in one video can easily be used to create future montages. A short-form video on one platform can easily be reposted on another, without needing to make any major changes. And long-form content can easily be sliced up to create endless pieces of short-form video.

Put simply: video content won't just improve your growth, it will also save you time.

A lot of people hold back from creating videos because they don't feel ready. They don't have the right tools. They don't feel confident. And they're not sure what to say.

So let's break down what you *actually* need to harness video effectively...

Structure your video

The concept for your video will make or break it. You can have the fanciest set-up possible, but if the content of the video isn't clear, it's unlikely to hold people's attention and communicate what you want it to.

- An impactful video:
- Delivers one clear message.
- Hooks you in at the start.
- Follows a storytelling structure.

1 Deliver one clear message

Before creating any piece of video content, ask yourself one question: what am I trying to achieve with this video?

Are you sharing a certain tip? Telling a story? Showing your product? Creating a relatable or entertaining moment? Particularly with short-form content, where you've got seconds not minutes at your disposal, having one clear goal is key.

Cramming five tips into a sixty-second video will likely leave the viewer more confused and overwhelmed than they were at the start. And remember: we're sharing content to give people value, so let's ensure we stick to that.

One of my favourite points to bring up here is from Kirsty Hulse, confidence expert and experienced public speaker, who says: 'Don't speak to impress, speak to inspire. Remove the focus from HOW CAN I LOOK SMART to how can I make people feel or do something differently.'

Each time I hear that reminder, my shoulders drop and suddenly the misplaced pressure I'm putting on myself to 'perform' is replaced by a far more valuable and exciting intention: to inspire.

2 Hook people in

The first few seconds of your video are critical, as it's when viewers are deciding whether to keep watching or not.

With that in mind, you should use a hook at the beginning of your video to pique people's interest and give them enough context so that they're encouraged to keep watching. A hook could be...

- 'Let me tell you about my biggest health mistake...'
- 'Ready to make your home less IKEA and more you? This tip will change it all...'
- 'Last week we got some bad news. Here's what happened...'

- '75% of businesses would make more sales if they changed this one thing...'
- 'Is modern dating dead? Let's ask some people...'
- 'Come with me while I write my book in a week...'

Think of your hook like the title of an article: it exists to grab attention and lead into the body of the content.

3 Follow the storytelling structure

The most engaging and effective videos contain three key components:

An opening clip to hook your viewer and give a hint at what's to come.

One clear message in the middle, whether it's a tip, story or piece of news.

A conclusion at the end to encourage viewers to take action as a next step.

Tools for creating video content

What if you already had the tools you need for creating video content? It's likely in your pocket, on your desk or maybe it's what you're reading this book on... your phone.

Phone

While you may look at others with fancy set-ups and expensive equipment and want to strive for the same level of quality, you don't necessarily need to begin there. In fact, we're seeing a rise in consumers preferring lower-quality content filmed on a phone over the fancy output of a film crew. Why? Because it feels more

> **TIP**
> To help you follow this structure, write out a rough plan for your clips and bullet points for your script beforehand. This will make your content easier to film and edit and ensure you're keeping the correct flow.

authentic. Your video content is not about creating a movie-worthy clip, it's about engaging with people and keeping it authentic. Sure, your big launch video or event round-up may work best using a camera, but when it comes to short-form social content, a phone is your best friend.

Here are some other tools you may find useful:

Microphone

While a phone's microphone can do just fine, if you're looking to improve quality, are filming in a noisy area or are standing further away from the phone when filming, investing in a mic will make a difference. Just search 'lavalier mic for phone' online and you'll find a variety of options to pick from.

Tripod

For filming behind-the-scenes footage or B-roll (for example, clips of you working or packing an order), a tripod may help you get the right angles. Whether you need an overhead tripod to capture your hands, a standing tripod for putting on the floor or a mini tripod to help you create content on the go, this will speed up your filming process and ensure your clips are the best format.

One of the best 'DIY' tripod tips I've ever seen is from my friend and content marketing expert Rachel Waring: 'Often we overthink video, and think we need all sorts of fancy equipment before we can create high-quality content, but that couldn't be further from the truth. It can be as simple as grabbing a tin can and strapping your phone to it with an elastic band to give you a makeshift tripod. Resourcefulness will get you far!'

Prop up your phone against a can, secure it with an elastic band, and you've got yourself a free and effective tripod!

Lighting

One of the simplest changes that will make your video content more engaging is the lighting. You may have the best video concept ever, but if the clips are so badly lit we can barely see your face or the visual you're showing, you'll lose people's attention. A free and impactful step is to make sure you're facing natural light when you film. For example, if recording a talking video, stand in front of a window.

If you're lacking natural light or simply want to improve the quality, you can invest in something like a ring light or a box light to brighten up your videos. I have a ring light on my desk that I can easily switch on any time I'm recording video. It definitely helps when I'm not feeling my best!

Editing your video

So you've recorded your video, now it's time to edit! The complexity of your edit totally depends on the video in question, but I can confidently say that most edits are simpler than you think. Particularly for short-form video, you'll likely be following these steps:

1. Cut the clips down. Remove any mistakes or extra content at the start or end.
2. Add the clips together. If your video involves multiple clips, put them in the correct order.
3. Add any text or voiceover needed.
4. Optional: edit the colouring of the videos.

> **TIP**
> if you're creating a lot of video content via a phone, you may find it easier to invest in a specific phone for this use. That way, everything business-related is in one camera roll and you don't need to worry about using up storage on a personal phone.

Oh, and be sure to add text! Jess Wreford, Chief Creative Officer at Antler Social, says: 'Captions are not only important for accessibility, but will also ensure people who watch your videos with the sound off can still engage. On-screen text can also allow you to add extra descriptive parts to the video (for example, in a recipe video, you can have the ingredients pop up on screen so watchers can screenshot them). Watchers are constantly wanting to be entertained, so utilizing the addition of captions and on-screen text is a great way of keeping people immersed throughout.'

Many free apps will help you do these steps. Another option is to edit within the social media platform it's being posted to. If you're adding text, doing this in the font that is native to the platform it's being posted on will likely increase the engagement.

Confidence

So we've got the structure, we know our tools... we're ready to create content, right? On paper, yes, we have what we need, but there's something beneath the surface that can get in our way: a lack of confidence.

A lot of video content requires us to speak to camera, record a voiceover or just be in a clip, which can bring up feelings of fear. We worry what people will think, whether we're good enough, if it's cringy... and while I doubt any of your video-related fears will ever be true, they're valid. And they're often what hold people back from showing up in this way.

When I first started talking to camera seven-plus years ago I remember feeling so scared, but nowadays it feels like second nature. I share that to demonstrate that you rarely feel ready, but when you take messy action, you improve.

One of my favourite reminders for people who feel intimidated by something new is that the best way to learn and improve is to do it. Embrace the messy action and give it a go. Here are three reminders that may help you with that:

Start with baby steps

If you've never recorded video before, going out onto the streets of London to interview strangers probably isn't a good first step.

How about we begin with something a little closer to your comfort zone? You could try recording a voiceover to put on top of other clips, sharing a photo of yourself just to get used to bringing 'you' into your content, or just recording a video for it never to be posted. The sooner you can take action, the sooner your confidence will grow.

Re-record if you need to

If you ever see my video content on socials, you can safely bet that you're watching take number 2, 3 or even 7 of that shot. It's okay to re-record! I often find the first time I record something is less about getting it right and more about trying out the concept and finding the right script. If you get it right first go, amazing! But if you need a few takes to land on something you're happy with, that's totally fine. Practice doesn't make perfect (we're not aiming for perfect!), but practice does make progress.

Imagine you're speaking to one person

Content is a conversation and video format shouldn't change that. Sometimes we can get in our heads and imagine we're speaking to thousands of people at once – something that may be true but won't help you to speak in an engaging way. Any time I'm talking into my phone or a camera, I like to imagine one person on the other side of it. I'll pretend I'm on FaceTime with someone or visualize one of my clients watching the clip. This not only helps me to relax but it also helps me remember to communicate as I usually would. So I use eye contact, speak to one person rather than a collective and I use my facial expressions.

Slow down

A final tip is to slow down. Our fear can sometimes lead us to speak a million miles an hour when on video, something that will instantly lose people's engagement. So take a breath, leave pauses between sentences and speak slower than you would normally.

Successful marketing is less about the tools you have

and more about the action you take.

Summary / Action

Key learnings:

1. You find your voice by using it.
2. Video content is a powerful tool for engaging new audiences and staying modern with your marketing approach.
3. Both short-form and long-form videos have their own purposes.
4. Impactful videos deliver one clear message.
5. Starting your video with a hook and following the storytelling structure will keep viewers engaged.
6. Your phone is all you need, but if you want to upgrade in quality you can look into microphones, tripods and lighting.
7. Fear is a normal experience when creating video. Take baby steps and lower the pressure.

Action steps:

- Explore how video content could work for your marketing.
- Determine which tools you need to get started.

Lucy Hitchcock of Partner in Wine

When Lucy Hitchcock founded Partner in Wine, the brand making wine cool again through insulated wine accessories, she had no clue how pivotal video content would be to her success. Let's dive in...

When starting Partner in Wine, how did you approach video content? Did you immediately see the benefit or was there a moment you realized it?

I've never actually been that good with video content. However, when I started documenting the journey of starting PIW on my social media, I realized that people loved being involved. So when Reels and TikTok suddenly burst onto the never-ending list of things you're expected to do to market your business, I figured that would be a good place to start. I'd seen loads of businesses blow up on TikTok and sat for months scrolling, watching – I suppose you could call it lurking – obsessively analyzing what made a good video. I'd posted maybe a dozen times (badly, I might add) before I got my first viral hit.

Tell me about your first viral video, how it performed, why you think it did so well and the immediate results.

The first viral video was titled 'I started a business during the pandemic'. It told the story of the first seven months of my business, from packing in my parents' front room, to moving into a fulfilment centre, and hitting my first 10K month. I posted it at 11am having spent hours making it, still really not understanding how TikTok worked, and just before I threw my phone out of the window in despair, I posted it. At around 6pm that evening I noticed I was getting a few more sales than normal but nothing out of the ordinary. The next morning, I woke up at 7.30am, and I had thousands of new Instagram followers, but most importantly I'd made thousands of pounds worth of sales already. I was frantically trying to work out where the sales were coming from, as sales notifications were pinging through every single second. When I realized it was TikTok, I had gone from about 100 followers to over 7,000 in less than 24 hours, and I had hundreds of people on my website. That single video caused me to make my first five-figure sales day, increased my sales by 1700% overnight, and I sold a unit every two minutes for three days consecutively until I'd totally sold out.

But it didn't stop there...

What has video done for your business?

The aftermath of that single video, and all of my other videos since, has been immeasurable.

I've not once reached out to a wholesaler; they've all come to me: Selfridges, Liberty London, Oliver Bonas, Urban Outfitters, Daylesford.

I've been featured in pretty much every press publication you could think of, and my story has been told by the BBC, *Business Insider*, *Heat* magazine, Sheerluxe, *The Sun*, *The Express*, and many more.

I've sold well over 15K units, and have a six-figure business.

How do you navigate the trolling or fear that can come with video content?

The only time I do get 'hate' is on viral videos – people don't like your voice, they don't like the price, they don't like the product. They troll because they will never buy from you so there's no point replying – I ignore it and usually someone who supports your business will argue back for you. Getting negative reactions is a risk you take, but if you're really affected by it then just don't read the comments. When I first went viral I asked my friend to monitor it and send me the nice supportive comments, which made me feel better until I learnt to ignore the negative ones!

Your top three tips for a compelling video:

1. Educate, entertain and inspire: Always make sure your video falls into one of these three categories. You don't always have to talk about your products, so ask yourself what else does your business stand for, and what can you teach or how can you entertain or inspire your ideal customer?

2. Make them as short and snappy as possible: People have really short attention spans, so even when I'm making ninety-second videos, they always chop between one sentence and the next, zoom in and out, and use changes in angles. Good editing keeps people watching.

3. Don't get complacent and always keep it real: I'm always asking myself how I can level up my videos, get out of old habits (even when I know some formats work well) and create new and interesting videos.

'Stocked in Selfridges with a six-figure business, all thanks to video'

Left: New platforms can feel intimidating at first, but by adopting a mindset of experimentation, Lucy has diversified her reach and grown her business rapidly.
Right: People want to hear the story and the 'why' behind your business. By sharing this, Lucy reached almost a million potential customers, a virality that led to increased sales, wholesale opportunities and press features.

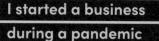

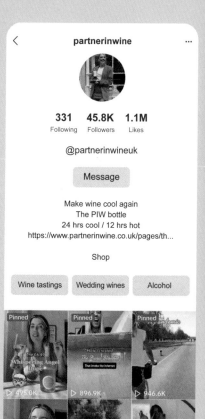

17.
Mastering storytelling

At the core of every engaging and effective piece of content sits one thing: a story. Stories take you on a journey, they humanize whatever is being shared, and they leave people feeling like they've been a part of the conversation.

The sooner you see each piece of content as a story and the more you can find ways to tell stories within your marketing, the more engaging your content will be. And a story can look many different ways.

- You could tell the story of a recent experience you had in order to share a specific tip or encouragement.
- You could tell the story of something you're developing or working on in your business right now.
- You could tell the story of what happened to a client or customer as a result of them buying from you.

Storytelling can take place in our captions, our videos, our website copy, our email drafts and so much more. So how do we tell a great story?

Master structure

At school I clearly remember being told that every story should follow the same structure, with a beginning, a middle and an end. There's not much I learned at school that helps me with my business today, but that tip is one exception. If you structure your content that way, you'll not only share something that's more engaging and effective, but also find it easier to create.

The beginning is your hook and intro – the moment to grab attention and set the scene.

The middle is the value of your content – delivering one key message (or multiple if it's long-form).

The end is your conclusion or call to action – what you want people to do or think about next.

This structure is particularly helpful when writing copy, as we can feel overwhelmed when sat with a blank caption or document. Decide what story you want to tell and consider how it can fit that structure.

- What do you need to say at the start to give context and get people interested?
- What is the main message or explanation you're delivering in the middle?
- And so it doesn't end abruptly, what is the call to action or conclusion you're leaving people with?

Content created in this way takes people on a journey.

Give context

When it comes to telling a great story, context is everything.

Ever found yourself speaking to an already established friend group and left feeling totally confused about what they were discussing? Or perhaps as a child you went to other family's houses and didn't get any of the jokes they shared?

That's because you don't have context – a key ingredient to ensuring people can understand and therefore fully engage with whatever you're sharing.

Giving context is about making sure your audience know the relevant information to help them understand your message.

The enemy of context is assumption.

We already know it, so we assume others do too. And that's an expensive assumption to make.

The most accessible stories give context. They set the scene at the start. They explain why this story is relevant. They fill you in on the backstory relevant to the story you're about to tell.

Use personal experience as the hook

Storytelling often involves introducing some form of personal experience, which is part of what make a story effective. However, assuming we want this content to provide value to our community, we want to be careful not to make the whole piece of content about us.

My favourite way to balance this is to use personal experience to hook people in and give an example they can relate to and make it about the reader/watcher/listener in the conclusion.

Let's look at some examples of this:

- You could discuss your recent challenge of trying to stay productive in the heat, and then end the post with three tips for those feeling the same way.
- You could share a statistic around your business growth and then conclude it with a couple of inspiring statements or encouraging reminders for those wanting to do the same.
- You could talk about a problem you used to face and why it frustrated you, and then share why your product or service could help those in a similar position.
- You could celebrate the fact that you're working remotely, before asking your community if it's something they'd want to do too.

By using yourself as the hook but then making it about them, you're creating an engaging and relatable piece of content that ultimately serves your community.

Telling your story

When telling your story, it can be hard to feel confident that you're clearly explaining what you do, while keeping it interesting for the listener. I know I sometimes dread introducing myself for this exact reason!

A simple structure can make all the difference. I spoke with Katie Briefel, marketing and storytelling expert, to better understand how we can tell our story in an engaging way and these are her suggestions:

- Start by setting up the status quo; for example, most deodorants are made with toxic chemicals.
- Then create a sense of conflict; for example, this has x impact on the environment and you.
- Finish by demonstrating your resolution; for example, so we came up with a unique solution that addresses this.

Summary / Action

Key learnings:

1. Every great piece of content follows the same structure of a story: a beginning, a middle and an end.
2. Giving context is key to ensuring people can engage with the stories you're telling.
3. Use a personal experience as the hook and then make it about the reader / viewer / listener in the conclusion.

Action steps:

- Try using the storytelling structure in a piece of your content.
- Reflect on the stories you could tell in your business to provide value and relatability to your community.

TIP
Notice how the content you consume uses storytelling to keep you engaged. The more you think about storytelling, the more you'll see how widely and repetitively it's used!

18.
Encouraging action and increasing sales

As we spoke about right at the start of this book, we want to see our marketing as a conversation, not a broadcast. That shift in perspective impacts a lot of how we create content. One of the biggest is that we want people to speak back and take action.

Our content shouldn't be about shouting our message from a stage and hoping somebody listens. It should be about sitting down with people and inviting them to both speak back and take action.

Action leads to sales

The ultimate action we want people to take is to buy our thing, right? That's at the final stage of the buyer's journey: decision.

But what if we looked at encouraging action throughout all the stages of the buyer's journey and increased our sales by doing so?

If the first and only action you encourage people to take is to buy now, you'll likely see a lack of conversion, and I'm not surprised. Nurturing an engaged community who are warm (that is, ready to buy) requires getting them to take action throughout their journey. This focus on action will help people to build a deeper connection with your business, signal to the platforms they're on that they want to see more of your content and, ultimately, get them used to engaging with you.

Alice Benham Dictionary
CTA, or call to action: when you invite people to take action off the back of a piece of content.

As we discussed in the previous chapter, ending your content with a CTA is a great way to conclude the message and invite them to take a step closer to your business. I would suggest that every single piece of content should include some form of call to action, so let's unpack the different types.

What CTAs to use?

The obvious call to action we all think about is the 'buy now' action. That is one way of inviting action, but if every post we share ends with the invitation to buy, your audience are likely going to start ignoring it and you'll also be missing out on more than 90% of your community.

What about all the people towards the start of their buyer's journey who aren't yet ready to buy?

We need to think about engaging with them too. What action do we want them to take? What next step would increase their engagement with your business?

Here are seven types of CTAs you can use in your content:

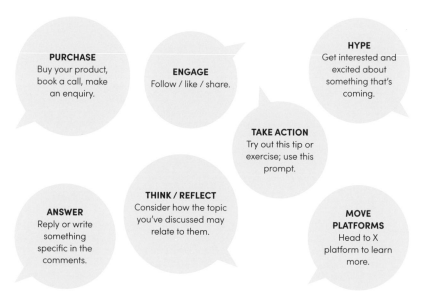

PURCHASE
Buy your product, book a call, make an enquiry.

ENGAGE
Follow / like / share.

HYPE
Get interested and excited about something that's coming.

TAKE ACTION
Try out this tip or exercise; use this prompt.

THINK / REFLECT
Consider how the topic you've discussed may relate to them.

ANSWER
Reply or write something specific in the comments.

MOVE PLATFORMS
Head to X platform to learn more.

These calls to action should be used across all of your content to nurture a community of engaged and action-taking people.

Tips for writing CTAs

Make it compelling

Simply saying 'link in bio to buy' or 'let me know what you think in the comments' isn't enough. Give people a reason to want to take the action. Better examples would be 'to transform your wardrobe today, click the link in the bio to browse' or 'I'm curious to know if you've experienced this before and what helped you. Comment below – I'm all ears!'

Link it to the content

A call to action is designed to blend seamlessly with the piece of content it sits at the end of, so make sure it matches. For example, if you're referencing a topic that you've shared more about on another platform, use a 'move platform' CTA, or if you're showing the behind the scenes of a new offer, you'll probably want the CTA to be 'join the waitlist here'. Put simply: make it make sense.

Mix it up

Always using the same CTA will turn into background noise and either bore or become invisible to people. Make sure you're making full use of the different types of CTAs available to you and keep your audience on their toes. This will also ensure you're speaking to various people at once.

Reward it

If you want people to take a piece of action like commenting or replying, be sure to acknowledge and reward that by responding back. Leaving people hanging is a sure-fire way to leave them uninterested in taking action again, so take notice when your community engages with you.

TIP
Don't be discouraged if you use a call to action and people don't follow it; you often need to be repetitive before people begin responding.

How to sell more

Alice Benham Dictionary
Selling: inviting your community to take action and buy your product or service.

Taking it back to our fish in the pond analogy, sales is when we pop in the net and give the fish a reminder that they can upgrade ponds.

I notice we can have a lot of resistance when it comes to sales and I believe the biggest reason for this is that we're looking at sales the wrong way. We're associating sales with ickiness, pressuring people to buy or getting rejected. While that may be true of some sales approaches, the type of selling we want to normalize is the opposite of all of those things.

It's value-driven, consensual and feels good on both sides. It's an opportunity and invitation, not a pressured moment.

How marketing and sales interact

One of the biggest factors that allows our sales to perform in this way is all the other work we're doing in our marketing. Sales and marketing are sometimes seen as different functions, but I see them as a tag team.

Marketing > Sales

Marketing is about connecting with people, inviting them in, building their understanding of what you do, getting to know your business.

Sales is simply what happens when we then invite those people to buy.

Sales can feel icky when we don't have marketing in place, because then we're trying to take people the whole way through the buyer's journey in one moment. Ever had a cold call try to sell you something despite you not knowing the company or even expressing an interest in their offer? Yeah, that's what sales without marketing can look like.

So already, by implementing a marketing strategy, you are proactively contributing to your sales. You are sowing seeds, often subconsciously, which may down the line grow into sales.

Two types of sales

There are two key ways that we can sell within our marketing, and it comes down to your cadence:

Launch + Ongoing

Launch

Selling a limited number or for a limited time; there is a hype period beforehand and a very focused window for sales.

Ongoing

The offer is always available so clients and customers are able to buy or enquire any time.

Your business may use one of these approaches or a blend of the two; it depends on what you sell and how you want to sell it. Each approach has its own pros and cons, so consider which will work best for you and experiment if you're unsure.

Eight steps to sales

Although we're not forcing anyone to buy, there are steps we can take to help encourage more conversion within our marketing. It's easy to sit back and wait for the sales to come in of their own accord, but let's be proactive in increasing our sales.

TIP
List out your offerings and define whether they are sold through a launch or an ongoing basis. This clarity will help you understand how to sell them in a more intentional way.

1 Nail your messaging

We've discussed this point already, but I'm bringing it back up because it is key to sales: people buy impact, not format. A lot of businesses make the mistake of selling their features – what the product is, how the service works, what's included. Although that information is relevant, it isn't compelling. People buy something because of the impact it will make on them and their lives – how it will make them feel, look, achieve. When you're selling, be sure to bring that into your messaging. Great copy explains how the format leads to the impact, so check that your sales emails, ads and website do just that.

2 Show, don't tell

What if I told you that your content could be selling subtly, without it ever feeling that way? That's the magic of showing, not telling. Telling people what we do, how it works, who it's for, might feel salesy and boring, right? But showing people those things by documenting and storytelling... now we're talking. When you show people what you sell, you're sowing seeds of information around your offer without them even realizing it. Then, when they're ready to buy or given the opportunity to, they'll already be part-way through the buyer's journey.

3 Create a clear process to buy

Confused people don't buy, so we need to make sure the steps to purchase are simple. Have you ever sat down in a restaurant and been confused about whether you wait for a waiter, order at the counter or scan a QR code? Or perhaps found a checkout process so clunky you just gave up? A confusing or unclear process creates resistance, which will lower your conversion.

If you're product-based, e-commerce analyst and author Ian Hammersley suggests you:

Address customer anxieties
By implementing measures such as guarantees, warranties and a clear returns policy you'll alleviate any concerns and increase confidence in making a purchase.

Build trust and credibility

Building trust is essential for e-commerce success, which you can do by showcasing evidence from customers and third-party credible sources, such as testimonials, reviews and trust seals, to reinforce the credibility of your brand.

4 Create a reason to buy

Your customer needs a reason to buy today, this week or this month. This includes implementing time-limited promotions, exclusive deals or other incentives to drive conversions.

If you're service-based and doing sales calls I'd suggest you:

- Create one clear enquiry point for prospective clients.
- Ensure the enquiry call is long enough to have a proper discussion.
- Stay in control but keep it conversational. You'll want to discuss 1) where they're at, 2) their goals and challenges and then finally 3) how your service could help them.
- End the call with an understanding of their thoughts and a clear next step for both of you.

5 Create stepping stones

I want you to think of your buyer's journey a little like stepping stones for a moment, with each step being a different platform or action people can take as they move from free content to purchasing from you.

Sometimes people are struggling to convert because their stepping stones look a little like this:

Instagram	Podcast		£2,000 service

The lack of stepping stones between free and paid means that your community have to make a pretty big leap of trust and interest to buy your thing. Something we can do to minimize this is fill in the gaps with free or entry-level offers:

Instagram	Podcast	Free workshop	£200 one-off session	£2,000 service

By adding in those two additional offers, we've shortened the leap between stepping stones and helped people to build trust and trial our work in a more low-risk way, likely increasing conversion to the full service.

6 If launching, generate waitlists

When launching something that has limited access, one of the simplest ways to increase conversion is to utilize a waitlist. A waitlist is an email list you set up specifically for those who are interested in buying and want to get first access. As we've already discussed, email is a powerful tool for conversion, so by gathering your most relevant people via email you can sell to them in a much more intentional way. You'll want to offer them first access and perhaps a discount or bonus for being on the waitlist, and make sure you're promoting it heavily when you're in the pre-launch phase.

I personally love using waitlists for launches; they allow you to sell to those who are interested and leave it at that.

7 If ongoing, create a rhythm to selling / know your availability

When we're selling something that's always available, we can easily go to the extremes of either selling all the time or not at all. It's the latter I see most commonly; because we can always be selling it, there's no structure that makes sure we do.

That's where bringing in a rhythm to the way you sell can help. A sales rhythm creates peaks and troughs for your ongoing sales, so you are clear on when to actively sell and when to let sales happen by themselves. There are a few ways you can do this:

- Identify your key sales periods. It's likely that your product or service has 'hot spots' in the year. Whether it is related to the seasons or celebration days, identify the times when it makes most sense for you to push sales and let your content follow.
- Set your availability. If you sell your services, knowing how many clients you have capacity for and advertising formal spaces will make it easier for you to promote your slots. For example, if you have two new client spaces per month you then have clearer messaging, will encourage your community to book up in advance and you'll then have a sales focus within each month.

- Offer limited bonuses or discounts. Urgency and scarcity are the primary reasons for people to click 'buy', so explore if there are ways you could introduce limited offers to drive conversion.

8 Be consistent

Data suggests that people need to hear a sales message at least seven times before taking action, so it's really important we keep selling, even when it feels like nobody is listening.

One of my favourite encouragements here is to 'sell through the silence', something Elizabeth Stiles, a fashion brand consultant, once shared:

'It's easy to feel disheartened when you don't see results straight away, so hold your nerve and sell through the silence! Most people assume that they're putting people off when actively selling their offer, but it's helpful to imagine that you're actually increasing their level of certainty that your offer is right for them. Every time you actively sell online, you're simply moving the right people one step closer to the checkout!'

Finding a way of selling that feels good to you isn't a nice-to-have extra, it's fundamental to you being effective and consistent in your sales. Take on board any of the tips I've shared that feel relevant to you and use them in a way that feels good to you.

Summary / Action

Key learnings:

1. We can and should encourage more than purchasing action in our content.
2. There are seven different styles of CTA for us to use.
3. It's important to link the CTA to the content, use a variety and make the CTA compelling.
4. There are two ways to sell: ongoing and launch.
5. Marketing and sales can work together to drive effective and value-driven conversion.
6. We can't control our sales, but we can influence them.

Action steps:

- Experiment with bringing more CTAs into your content, noticing what your community responds best to.
- Take an action step to improve your sales strategy.

19.
Ethical, accessible and inclusive marketing

I remember at school being taught about rights and responsibilities. The concept was pretty simple: you get access to rights and in exchange should upkeep certain responsibilities.

This is kind of how I view the topics we're looking at in this chapter.

We have the ability (or right) to utilize free platforms to grow our businesses. We get to be discovered by new people, nurture community, spread our message and ultimately generate sales. Pretty cool, right?

That ability (or right) comes with a few responsibilities, though. Responsibilities to show up in a way that does good.

I want to clarify that while I believe these things should be mandatory, they are merely suggestions. Of course there are government laws and platform policies you have to abide by, but what I'm talking about here are more like good practices. Ways of showing up that I believe will make business, the online space and ultimately the worlds we operate in better.

I mean, who doesn't want that?

Why I commit to value-driven business

Before getting into the details, I want to share why I personally think 'doing good' matters. To let you behind the curtain, this chapter didn't actually exist in my chapter plan or book outline. I only realized as I was finishing writing the last chapter that while I'd touched on my beliefs around value-driven marketing, there wasn't a dedicated chapter about this topic, despite it being one of the topics I'm most passionate about.

I wonder if I missed it off the initial plan because A) my knowledge bias makes me forget that not everyone thinks in this way and

B) I'm always a little nervous to touch on the subject out of fear of getting it wrong. So now those things are out of the way, let's talk about it.

Value-driven business is something I committed to in the very early days in my business, and it came from experiencing first-hand what the opposite of it looks like. When I started out as a naive but enthusiastic seventeen-year-old, I quickly found myself working with companies who cared about one thing and one thing only: sales. Everything was looked at through the lens of this goal, and there was little to no conversation or consideration around what else was important to us. People weren't seen as people; they were seen as potential income. And the values these companies shouted about online were very much lacking in their internal culture. I couldn't put words to it, but it felt icky.

A similar feeling was triggered for me when I began to grow my own business online and looked to others for inspiration. Like many of us do when trying something new, I mirrored the behaviour of others but quickly felt uncomfortable about the tactics and strategies I was following. I also found myself feeling intimidated and overwhelmed by the content flying around that promised me I could make £100K in two minutes or told me that for the small price of £25,000 I too could learn their 'secrets' to success.

It took a bit of time and experimentation before I realized that my 'icky' feeling coming up in all of those scenarios was actually my values being triggered. I cared about doing business a certain way and each of these scenarios was the opposite of what felt right to me.

Then was born my love for value-driven business. To try and create one. To surround myself with them. And to help them grow.

Alice Benham Dictionary
Value-driven business: a profitable company run in a way that treats people well and honours the specific values of the team or owner

As we talked about back in Chapter 4, your values are unique to you and should act as a compass for your business: a central clarity you come back to, helping to guide your decisions as a business owner.

For me, my values come into every part of what I do and bring two big benefits:

1 I feel really good about my business

We spend most of our time working, so surely we deserve to feel good about what we're doing and how we do it? I realize neither of my businesses is saving lives (I'll leave that to my doctor brother!) but I feel really proud that I'm taking action to treat others well, *while* I pursue my own success.

2 My people have a greater trust with and connection with me

I used to think being value-driven meant sacrificing my potential growth, but now I can see that the two aren't mutually exclusive. My value-driven marketing is one of the biggest reasons my community have a connection with and loyalty to my work. It humanizes me, draws in others with similar values and gives people something to remember.

If you're feeling a bit stuck on where to begin or what value-driven marketing even looks like, there are two key topics I want to talk around: **ethical marketing** and **accessible marketing**. From where I'm standing, those are the primary areas we should be thinking about and taking action within. So let's unpack them.

Ethical marketing

An interview with Karen Webber, small business marketing strategist.

What is ethical marketing? How do you define it?

Ethical marketing for me is about helping people make informed purchasing decisions when it comes to the things you sell. It's marketing with integrity, which means being honest, transparent and clear in what you share with potential buyers and in doing so being a responsible business owner who doesn't just chase profit, but always considers the impact we have on people and the planet.

It's the opposite of what we're often taught around traditional marketing, where the focus is on manipulative approaches such as creating artificial demand and FOMO, and using psychological tricks to lure people into buying.

Why should we aim to be ethical in our marketing practices?

Put simply, because our actions and operations have an impact beyond our own businesses.

Our global economy is rife with inequality. Oppressive systems really only work in favour of a small group of players at the top who thrive while there's a growing wealth gap and incredible amounts of waste, discrimination, exploitation, displacement and fear.

At the core of this is an economy that relies on our insatiable appetite for more, which is fuelled by manipulative marketing.

If all businesses did ethical marketing, the whole world would change. We'd have empowered consumers who make better, more conscious purchasing decisions, which would be better for both individuals and the planet.

And it's not just because it's a good thing to do; it's simply good business to treat the people who might buy from us really well. And people are noticing. Increasingly, they want to buy from businesses whose values align with theirs, who they can trust to act in their best interests, who put planet and people before profit.

They also increasingly see through unethical behaviour and will call it out. Nothing erodes trust faster than thinking you're being lied to or being pressured or tricked into buying things, and with social media giving everyone a platform, these practices won't remain hidden forever.

What are the different ways we can be ethical in our approach? What can this look like in practice?

It starts with a commitment to doing better and an awareness of your current practices...

Put the person before the sale. Help the people who might buy from you make the best choice for *their* needs, rather than manipulating them to do what you want them to do.

Be honest. Don't make exaggerated claims, don't say something is exclusive or limited if it isn't really; that's called fake scarcity. Give people the details they'll need to make an informed decision.

Look through their lens. Focus on your ideal buyers and assess your marketing from their perspective. Do you offer them what they *really* need? Is your marketing honest, clear and transparent? Is there anything that could be misleading or confusing?

I would also suggest looking at the work of The Ethical Move, the global movement for ethical marketing.

Final encouragement:

There's no list of rules to follow, and while there are guiding principles, ultimately it is about people asking themselves whether they are doing marketing in a way that empowers people to make the best decisions for them as buyers.

In my experience it really helps to learn out in the open and in community with others. The more we talk about this with other business owners and collaborate in learning, the better our chances of changing the trajectory of marketing and having a huge collective positive impact on the world.

I'm sure that we can figure this out together, and in doing so we can reach a critical mass of ethical marketers who can change the world!

Accessible and inclusive marketing

An interview with Ettie Bailey-King, inclusive and accessible communication consultant.

What is inclusive marketing? How do you define it?

I define inclusive marketing as marketing content that's accessible, specific, representative, accurate and respectful, whoever we are. Mainstream marketing content doesn't represent, include or work for everyone. Just a few examples of people who aren't always served by marketing content would be:

Disabled people. As few as 3% of websites are actually accessible for disabled users!

People of colour. All too often, people of colour don't get to see themselves visibly represented in marketing content, or they're there, but heavily stereotyped.

Women. A huge bulk of marketing content targets women, but not always in inclusive ways. Adverts have long presented women's bodies as sources of shame. Think of razor adverts showing people shaving already-shaved legs, because hair on our legs would just be too taboo.

Trans, non-binary and gender-non-conforming people. Language such as 'ladies and gentlemen' or 'both genders' suggests there are only two genders. But there are many, not just two!

LGBTQIA+ people. Being heterosexual is pretty common, but it's not the only sexual orientation. Often, marketing copy assumes that people have a spouse or partner of the opposite gender.

Older people. Reductive stereotypes about older people often show up in marketing content. Maybe we say 'our product is so simple, your grandma could use it!', which implies older people are out of touch.

Why should we aim to be inclusive in our marketing practices?

To put it another way: why wouldn't we want to be inclusive? Why would we not want to create content that works for disabled, neurodivergent, queer, Global Majority (people of colour) people, and other people from minoritized communities?

If you're just chasing recognition, your audience can tell. A brand that lives and breathes its values, like Patagonia, is instantly recognizable. If you're trying to look progressive but you don't believe in it, people will quickly see past your Black History Month Instagram post or your rainbow-coloured logo.

Don't do it to win awards or get more customers. Do it because it's right.

What are the different ways we can be inclusive in our approach? What can this look like in practice?
Inclusive marketing looks different everywhere. It could look like:

A wedding planner whose website shows a joyful mixture of clients with different racial backgrounds, sexual orientations, genders, body types, disabilities and more.

A marketer who formats her emails using a clear, readable typeface in a large font size, always checks for colour contrast, and includes alt text and image descriptions.

A photographer who makes their sales page short, clear and to the point. They use short, simple words, sentences and paragraphs, knowing that it helps neurodivergent, disabled, anxious, tired and distracted readers.

Depending on the business you run, inclusive marketing content might mean different things. Maybe you:

- Watch out for stereotypes and patronizing or judgemental language.
- Create screenreader-friendly content by using meaningful subheadings and using emojis sparingly.
- Use clear, literal, simple English.
- Are specific when talking about minoritized identities (for example, race, gender, sexual orientation).
- Represent diversity in your images, in the stories you tell, in the brands and individuals you partner with, in your suppliers.

If you're unsure where to begin, follow content creators who are different to you: different disabilities, races, genders, sexual orientations and more. You'll be entertained and informed, and you'll also pick up many ideas for who might be under-served in your marketing content right now, and how you can better serve them.

Remember, no one expects you to get everything right! You can't be perfect, and it would be ridiculous to try to be. I spend all day researching inclusive and accessible communication, and I still make mistakes. There's nothing wrong with getting something wrong, being corrected, and then changing it. If you try to make your website more accessible, or your language more inclusive, you will probably slip up. That's totally fine! Just keep going.

You'll never be 'perfect', because perfection doesn't exist.
When starting the conversation around a topic like this, I often notice we can feel overwhelmed by the need to do better. Our desire to do good morphs into a fear that we won't do enough good, that people may tell us off or that we won't be perfect at it.

I get it, because I often feel a similar way. It can be tempting to look at this work in extremes, thinking we either do everything perfectly (which is impossible) or just stay comfortable and unaware, as we currently are.

But I want us to value progress over perfection, as the campaigner and entrepreneur Sulaiman R. Khan puts it. To identify what changes we can make, slowly and messily, to take steps towards a more value-driven business.

The nature of value-driven is that it looks different for every-one, so there really isn't a universal code for us all to abide by. What's most important is that you connect to what matters most to you and be okay with experimenting and figuring it out as you go.

We'll never be perfect, but if we all do our best, I'm pretty excited to think about how we'll be raising the bar of what value-driven marketing means.

Conclusion

Come back to these chapters any time you need to remind yourself of some practical tips and strategies.

Now we've got your plan nailed, let's finish by putting it into action...

Summary / Action

Key learnings:

1. Value-driven marketing is about taking action that aligns with your personal values.
2. The more we let our values influence our action, the better our businesses will feel and the more growth we'll see as a result.
3. Ethical marketing is about helping people make informed purchasing decisions.
4. Inclusive marketing is about creating content that's accessible, specific, representative, accurate and respectful for everyone.
5. Being value-driven isn't about being perfect or following a standard set of rules; it's about making messy progress towards what matters to us.

Action steps:

- Clarify your values as a business owner: what do you stand for?
- Review your past marketing efforts: how can you take action to be more ethical, inclusive and accessible in your approach?

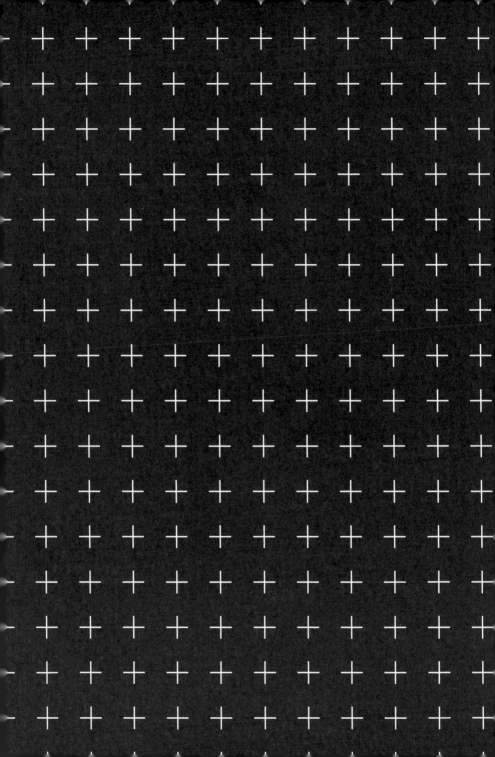

PART III

Take action

Action

The success of your marketing strategy is determined by your ability to implement it consistently.

So let's explore messy action and learn how to take it.

20.
Why implementation is the most important step

There's no point creating a marketing strategy if you're not going to implement it. There, I said it.

So often I see people getting it wrong. Their goal is to *have* a marketing strategy, when in actual fact our goal should be to *use* one.

If you're planning to put the book down here and just 'give it a go', can I kindly suggest you sit back down and keep reading. I know you've learned the practical stuff and will want to start trying it all out (love your enthusiasm!) but it's important we conclude your strategy with a conversation around action. Otherwise you may well have wasted your time doing all the other work.

Why? Because action is the only thing that will grow your business.

The marketing goals you defined at the start of the book – *you know the ones* – will only be achieved if you take action. Learning is cool. Planning is fun. Strategizing feels productive. But none of those things will achieve your goals. Only your external action will.

Internal versus external action

To be even more explicit, what I'm talking about here is external action; that is, the tasks that involve showing up, creating content and, in simpler terms, doing the thing.

Up until this point you've done a whole lot of internal action. You've expanded your expertise, gained invaluable clarity, developed plans and mapped out strategies. That internal action is something to celebrate, because it will absolutely help you achieve your goals. But it's only effective when followed up with external action.

I notice that many of us, myself included, have a comfort zone in internal action. The learning, planning and clarifying feels good because it feels safe. Nobody sees it, judges or has the capacity to reject it.

That's a pretty normal mindset to have, but I want you to notice it and be careful of how and when it shows up for you. Sometimes, if we're not careful, we can use internal action as a way to distract ourselves from what we really need to do – the external stuff.

'I'll just refine my messaging one more time.'

'I need one more online course and then I'm good to go.'

'Let's revisit the plan before we put it into place.'

Any of those sound familiar?

Those are all classic cases of fear disguising itself in a logical way. Of course our brain is trying to stop us from doing the stuff that feels uncomfortable, so of course it's trying to come up with a way to stick in the comfort zone – with internal action.

Sadly I can't sit with you at your desk to help identify when you're ready to transition from internal to external action, but I have a feeling one of these reminders may help:

- The sooner you start taking external action, the more learnings you'll be able to have to improve the internal plans.
- Nobody ever feels ready... ever (take it from someone who has walked alongside thousands of people as they try new things!).

Messy, curious and consistent action

Now, I don't want you to commit to taking any old action. I want you to commit to taking messy, curious and consistent action.

Read those three words again for me: messy, curious and consistent.

Messy

You'll never feel ready and you'll likely never feel like you've done it perfectly, so lower the bar and get comfortable with messy action. The sooner you take it, the sooner you'll learn and grow.

Curious

Speaking of learning, we want to take action and be immediately curious about what we can take from it. Action breeds clarity and the best strategies come from experimentation, so look for the mix of results and lessons, and be open to the evolution that will come as a result.

Consistent

Showing up for one week never to be seen again won't do a thing for your marketing goals. Putting in the work and committing to consistency (especially before you see results!) is the only 'secret' to success I've ever come across.

What gets in the way of us taking action?

The reason that action is getting a whole section in this book isn't because it's a particularly complex topic (it's pretty self-explanatory when you think about it); it's because so many things get in the way of us and action:

- Fear of what others will think
- Limited time
- The possibility of rejection or failure
- Poor organizational skills
- Comparison to others
- Perfectionism

Each item on that list is a normal part of the experience but has a scarily effective way of messing up our action, often without us even being aware of it. So in the following chapters I'm going to walk you through what you can do not to avoid those problems, but to plan against them and limit their impact and to help you take action despite those issues.

TIP
Write 'I commit to messy, curious and consistent action' somewhere you'll see it regularly. Whether it be on your marketing strategy doc, office wall or laptop background, keep your commitment visible as a reminder to your future self.

You'll never feel ready,

so take
action with
what you
have and learn
as you go.

Summary / Action

Key learnings:

1. The success of a strategy comes down to how we implement it.
2. Many of us find it more comfortable taking internal action, which can sometimes be a distraction from taking external action.
3. Messy, curious and consistent action will lead to the most sustainable growth.
4. We're only human for letting problems like fear, lack of time and overwhelm interrupt our action taking.

Action steps:

- Write 'I commit to messy, curious and consistent action' somewhere you'll see it regularly.
- Reflect on when you've taken external action within your marketing before. What has got in your way?

21.
How to plan your marketing

'I don't have time' is a sentence I regularly hear from business owners. When I surveyed my community recently, over 85% listed a lack of time as the biggest reason they weren't achieving their marketing goals.

And while I get it – time can feel like the biggest enemy to progress – it's an unhelpful statement, because, put very simply, we can't magic up more time.

If I could do that, believe me I'd have made millions and be living it up in the Maldives right now. But I'm not; I'm writing this book in the communal gardens of my flat in south-west London, so let's drop that dream.

You're never going to get more time.

So how about we look at the way we're *using* our time?

More specifically, how we're using our time to implement our marketing strategies.

When people tell me that their biggest challenge is a lack of time, I'm always curious to explore what they're doing to get the most out of the time they have. We're not yet talking about time-saving strategies like automating and batch creating (see Chapter 24 for that) but instead the bare basics of having an implementation process.

Do you have an implementation process for your marketing?

Alice Benham Dictionary
Implementation process: a defined plan for how you'll put your marketing strategy into place.

Implementation process sounds fancy, doesn't it, but it's a basic and simple thing that many of us ignore. Yet it's something that will have a huge impact in the ease and output you experience.

One of the biggest reasons we struggle to implement our marketing strategy is because we don't make the time. Notice I didn't say *have* the time, I said *make* the time.

So often I see people with the best intentions, sure that they'll find time in their week to do their marketing work. But oops, Monday that urgent client thing came up, Tuesday it was sunny so we logged off early, Wednesday that other task took longer than expected, Thursday we received an email that made us spiral for an hour and oops, before we know it the task has been bumped off our to-do list every day and never given the time it needs.

We *have* to start prioritizing our marketing. That's easier said than done when we're often so busy 'in' the business, but your external action will never magically happen, so you have to make it happen. One of the biggest tools to help you will be outlining your implementation process.

By understanding your implementation process you'll be able to:

- Make time each day, week and month to carry out your key marketing tasks.
- Not get distracted by work that feels more urgent or gratifying.
- Save time on your marketing because there's a clear plan for you to follow.

So let's look at this process in more detail. There are three key steps, and these are steps that all of us will go through from having a marketing strategy to putting it into action:

Ideation > Planning > Creation

Defining the three separate tasks involved in bringing your marketing to life is much of what makes this process so helpful. I frequently see business owners trying to do all three implementation steps in one go, and that is a shortcut to overwhelm and inefficiency. We split the process up so we can understand our best way of doing that task and, most importantly, make time for it.

Step 1: Ideation

Before we begin any formal planning, we need to have some ideas! Ideation comes from the left side of your brain whereas planning comes from the right, which is why it makes sense to split these steps up.

Ideation is all about gathering ideas for your content and marketing. If we try to run straight into planning mode without any ideas in place we'll likely spend a long time looking at a blank spreadsheet... sound familiar?

The biggest lesson I've learned about getting ideas is that it doesn't happen when you force it. It happens when you're active.

- In the shower
- Speaking to a friend
- Packaging an order
- On a walk
- Bouncing ideas around with someone else
- Listening to a podcast
- Speaking to a client
- Engaging with your community

Your best ideas will likely come when you're not trying to think of any ideas at all, which is why this step is best done on an ongoing basis. By having a central place to jot down content ideas as you go, you'll slowly build up a bank of ideas to work from when it's time to plan.

Struggle for ideas? Here are a few ways I like to get my brain whirring:

- The conversations you're having with customers and clients: What questions are they asking? What are you bonding over? What have you shared?
- Past content: What resonated? What comments have people left or what messages have they sent?
- Your calendar: What have you been up to recently? How could a recent experience act as the base for a piece of valuable content?
- External tools: Websites like answerthepublic.com or ChatGPT can be great for giving you content ideas around a certain keyword or niche idea.

Step 2: Planning

This step is pivotal to marketing success, because it's when we actually create the plan of what we're going to be posting and doing.

The phrase 'If you fail to prepare, you prepare to fail' comes to mind.

But let me reword that for this instance: if you fail to plan, you'll find it pretty hard to consistently take action. Not as catchy, is it?

But the sentiment is there: planning is valuable. And finding a way of planning that works for you is vital.

You see, there isn't a one-size-fits-all approach to planning. If there was, we'd be ticking a box rather than creating an actually useful plan.

The purpose of a plan is to help you take action, so whether that plan looks different depending on the time of year or is unrecognizable from your friends' plans, that's okay. If it's helping you show up intentionally and consistently, it's doing the job.

There are three key questions to help you outline this part of your process:

1 When do you do it?

The length of time you plan for at a time completely depends on how your business operates best. You may find that you work best on short timelines, planning a week ahead at a time. Or you may have a team and therefore need to be looking at a month of marketing at once, further in advance.

Define the frequency of your planning and please put the time in your schedule. Wishing or hoping you'll magically find this time every X weeks is a sure-fire way to never do it. So make time in your schedule for a planning session.

TIP
When writing down an idea, try to link it to a platform or content pillar; that will help your future self to understand it better.

TIP
Sleep next to a notebook or order a waterproof shower notepad for when you get ideas at the least helpful times.

2 What are you planning?

The purpose of a marketing plan is to outline what you're doing, where and when.

- What you're doing = the content you'll be posting or the activity you'll be doing.
- Where you're doing it = the platforms or touch-points being used.
- When you're doing it = the date and (if relevant) time it'll happen.

The depth to which you want or need to plan completely depends on your approach, so consider what you will be specifically aiming to plan out during this session.

When planning content, I suggest you begin by checking in on your marketing goals and looking at the upcoming period. Define any specific focus areas. If you've got a big launch, key date or business event happening during that period, your marketing plan needs to know about it!

3 Where will you house it?

Having a central place to create, view and keep track of your marketing plan will make your life a whole lot easier. It will also mean any team members or external freelancers don't have to keep asking you questions all the time – the plan is their resource.

Where you house your plan is totally up to you. Whether it's in a spreadsheet, fancy organizational platform, whiteboard or array of Post-it notes, there's no right or wrong way to do it. The important thing is that it works for you.

Also, be open to changing the way you plan depending on the season. When I'm in launch mode, my plan is detailed and in a big spreadsheet. When I'm stepping back, it can be as simple as a list on my notes app or a couple of Post-its on my desk with rough ideas.

Stop looking for the perfect way to plan and start just making a plan.

Step 3: Creation

Once you've planned the content, it then needs creating! This final step is one that, like the planning, needs to be intentionally mapped out and put in the diary. I hate to think how many of my content plans have never made their way off of the spreadsheet and into the real world... don't be like me!

There are three things I want you to consider when deciding this step of your process:

1 Who is creating?

If you work solo you can answer this with a simple 'Me!', but if you have any form of a team, this question is important. Delegate content creation intentionally based on the skillset and capacity of each person involved.

2 When are we creating?

You have two ends of a spectrum here: batch create in advance or create five minutes before you post. Where do you sit on that spectrum? When will your content be created? Your answer may differ per platform.

3 How are we making it efficient?

We'll touch more on this in the penultimate chapter but what we want to think about here is the creation process itself and anything we can do to improve it. Think: repurposing long-form content, creating graphic templates, curating a library of images to pick from, and so on.

You do you, please

My biggest encouragement to you as you create and use your implementation process is to make it work for you. Because that's literally its whole job.

We can easily let perfectionism or comparison creep in when doing work like this, and assume every process has to be super shiny or we have to be amazing at following it. Wrong and wrong.

The best processes are a little scrappy. And the businesses who see most impact from a process let it flex – they change it, test it and don't get too hard on themselves if they mess up the process for a short while.

Here's some of my favourite hacks from other experts:

Keep it cohesive

'Getting clear on your message is the first step to creating a strong omnichannel presence. Once you have developed this message, it's important to consider how each platform feeds into your

buyer's journey and where you can create content overlaps. The best place to start is where you feel the most comfortable, as visibility is more important than perfection.'
Danielle Littler & Kieran Wallworth, founders of Attention Digital

Create a content machine

'To increase your output, create one piece of long-form content (audio, written or video) that acts as the lead and can then be turned into five-plus smaller pieces of content. So that this short-form content is more than just a tick-box exercise, consider what your specific goals are and ensure the lead content is repurposed to achieve this purpose. For example, podcast clips on social media drive traffic to the episode, blogs on the website are optimized for search engines.'
Sneha Morjaria, business operations consultant

Work with your drivers

'Anyone with an ADHD brain will know the absolute cold-sweat terrors of having to write a plan! *Where do I start? Where do I end? What's the point when I won't follow it anyway?* The key to successful planning for anyone with ADHD is to keep it simple, and understand the primary drivers of our neurodivergent brains: *interest, novelty, competition and urgency* (INCU).

For example, if you have to feel urgency to get anything done, adjust your time line to accommodate that. If you need competition to thrive, gamify your plan by allocating points to completed tasks or find a friend to work with and keep each other motivated! The only way you will get anything done is your way, and that's okay.'
Amanda Perry, ADHD business strategist and coach

Start with questions

'Coming up with social media ideas can be overwhelming, so simplify the process. Imagine your ideal customer or client and list three questions they need answered before they purchase from you. For example: When are you open? How much do you charge? What does X package include? Answer each one of those in a piece of content. That's three social posts right there.'
Rebecca Broad, organic social media manager

Summary / Action

Key learnings:

1. Having a plan will help you use the time you do have to show up consistently.
2. An implementation process outlines the three steps of external action: ideation, planning and creation.
3. Gathering ideas is best done on an ongoing basis.
4. Putting the time in your schedule to plan and create content is crucial.
5. The way you implement should be unique to your business and help you.

Action steps:

- Create an ideas bank for you to add your content and marketing ideas to on an ongoing basis.
- Put time in your schedule for steps 2 and 3 to plan and create your content.
- Reflect on what your best version of this process will look like.

22.
The power
of consistency

Messy, curious and <u>consistent</u> action.

Alice Benham Dictionary
Consistent marketing: putting in the work over a long
period of time.

Getting to connect with so many successful business owners and
entrepreneurs gives me a unique vantage point to learn from. I
regularly reflect on my clients, podcast guests and network,
pondering the question: what's their secret to success?

Between all of them, there's only one common trait I notice:
consistency.

You can have all the natural skill, charisma or contacts in the
world, but if you're not bringing consistency, you're not going to
see long-term and sustainable results. It's that simple.

Having said that, I often see consistency being misinterpreted.
We associate it with hustle culture, burnout and unnecessary
pressure. So let's do a little fact-checking...

SHOWING UP CONSISTENTLY	SHOWING UP CONSTANTLY
Showing up regularly over a long period of time.	Showing up every day.
Ensuring you show up from the right place.	Burning yourself out.
Taking less action that's more intentional.	Taking action for the sake of it.

Be consistent, not constant.

Not just because that's what will be most attainable for you, but
also because it will help your marketing growth.

Consistency builds trust

I won't sugar coat this: marketing growth can take time. You're unlikely to show up on day 1 and immediately have an engaged community who buy from you and share your business. It's far more likely that you'll have to put in work over time to reach that point.

Why? Because marketing is about building trust and trust takes time to build.

- It takes time for people to remember your business.
- It takes time for people to build their trust and relationship with you.
- It takes time for people to move through the buyer's journey.

True community takes time. So we need to show up, over time.

Consistency is about dropping the 'all or nothing' mindset and putting in the work, over time.

Think of it like a friendship. Imagine you meet a new friend on holiday. You spend every day together. Sharing meals. Going on adventures. Braiding each other's hair. It's pretty intense. But after two weeks you lose contact, potentially never to see each other again. Sure, you had a great time, but that's no way to build a long-term relationship.

Now the consistent approach would be different. Imagine seeing a friend on average once every couple of weeks. Sometimes less, sometimes more. But when you zoom out on the year, there's regularity. They show up. So you get to know them, trust them and recognize them when you come into contact. That's what we want to be aiming for.

Is your plan sustainable?

Perfect consistency doesn't exist, because it looks different to every single one of us. The most important factor to consider when being consistent is this: sustainability. An unsustainable plan is a shortcut to inconsistent action.

Alice Benham Dictionary
Unsustainable marketing: a level of output or quality that is unlikely to be able to be repeated over time, due to burnout or lack of resources.

When creating a marketing strategy – or any kind of plan, actually – it's easy to get carried away with ideas. We want to do all the things. We see others and want to keep up. We put pressure on ourselves to do the most. That ambition is great, unless it leaves us with a plan we can't actually implement over time.

Ideally this isn't something we check right at the end of creating a plan; it's an intention we hold right through the whole process. In order to plan sustainably we have to:

- Understand our capacity. How much time, energy and resources can we realistically commit to this?
- Create a plan with that capacity in mind.
- Continue to monitor our capacity, noticing if it changes and then making changes to the plan as a result.

Your definition of sustainable marketing will change over time, depending on the season of business and life you're in. So this is important to keep front and centre.

TIP
Look at your schedule and understand the exact amount of time you are willing and able to commit to marketing. The more specific you can be, the easier it will be to check your plan is sustainable.

Aside from ensuring the plan itself is sustainable, here are three steps that will help you take consistent action.

1 Choose self-discipline over motivation

Okay, buckle up, because this is a hard truth we rarely want to hear but often need to. <u>It is not enough to only take action when motivation strikes. We have to exercise self-discipline.</u>
Motivation is the moment when our emotional desire to do something is enough to make us just want to do it, naturally. It's lovely. It's also pretty hard to come by. If you only take action when you feel motivated, you're going to be wildly inconsistent. Motivation alone isn't enough...

That is why we have to exercise self-discipline. Self-discipline isn't about *wanting* to do something, it's about *choosing* to do it. Self-discipline rarely feels good in the moment, but will always benefit you in the long term.

I see this a little like a hybrid car. When there's fuel (motivation) in the tank then, yay, great, let's use it! But when that depletes, which it will, we've got a back-up reserve of battery power (self-discipline) to use instead.

| When motivation is high, use it! | When motivation is low... | ...use your self-discipline! |

For me, self-discipline kicks in when my desire for where I'm going outweighs my discomfort about getting there. Maybe I'm feeling a bit of fear, overwhelm or just plain tiredness. My brain's instinct is to listen to those feelings and benefit me in the short term. However, self-discipline's job is to choose long-term growth over short-term comfort, which is why it's so important you're clear on and excited about where you're going.

When your goals excite you, it's much easier to exercise self-discipline, because you know *why* you're doing it.

Here are a few practical tips for when you need to help yourself be self-disciplined:

- **Five-minute rule.** If you don't want to do a task, just pop a timer on for five minutes and commit to doing it for that long. Most of the time, once you're five minutes in, you've got into it, realized you're capable of doing it and feel motivated to continue.
- **Accountability.** Knowing that others are aware of our commitments will give us more skin in the game, immediately. Find others who can help keep you accountable or join co-working sessions that take the isolation away from work.
- **Track and reward.** Deep down, we're all children who desperately need a sticker chart to keep us on track. Consider making a visual tracker that helps you see your progress. If this will motivate you, give yourself a reward for a certain level of action.
- **Pomodoro method.** You'll work more efficiently by working in twenty-five-minute sprints with no distractions and then taking five-minute breaks. There are many timers online that you can use.

Side note: if you are feeling genuinely unwell, unsafe or burned out, this tip is not for you. Self-discipline is about pushing through surface-level feelings, not ignoring real underlying issues.

2 Let it be imperfect

One of the worst expectations we can place on ourselves is for perfection. Why? Because it doesn't actually exist and is therefore wildly unachievable. When we aim for 'perfect' consistency, we're taking on an all-or-nothing mindset that will result in something like this:

When we try and show up perfectly:

Whereas when we adopt imperfect consistency:

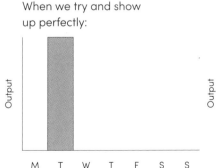

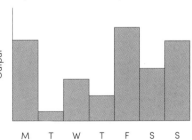

The mindset of imperfect action is about allowing for flex. Being okay with setbacks. And focusing more on what we can improve moving forwards. There are two scenarios I want to acknowledge here:

If you accidentally mess up

We're humans, business can be full of unexpected situations and life gets busy... so I can promise you that at some point you'll mess up. You'll stop showing up. You'll miss a deadline. You'll forget to do your planning. And that's okay.

It's not about beating yourself up for falling off the horse, and more about getting back on it and analyzing *why* you fell off, so you can support yourself moving forwards. When this happens, stop beating yourself up for 'failing' and start looking ahead to control what you can: your action.

If you need to step back

Despite harping on so much about the importance of consistency, there are times when the best thing to do is take a break.

- If you're feeling burned out.
- If you're feeling unsafe online.
- If something else has to take your priority.

Take a step back and do what you need to do.

Consistent marketing at the expense of your health or life isn't worth it. Sometimes you'll need to take a total break, but sometimes it could just be about lowering your output or minimizing the platforms you're on.

It sounds counterproductive, but the sooner you embrace imperfect consistency, the better you'll get at showing up.

3 Commit

This is my favourite consistency hack, particularly if you're doing something new. Define a non-negotiable minimum commitment period.

I did this back when I started my podcast. Knowing it would take a bit of time to find its feet, I decided I would do it for a year before deciding whether I should quit or not. That meant a year of consistent action, without letting myself get too bothered by the metrics.

And I'm so glad I did.

So many people deem that a strategy isn't working before they've given it time to succeed. That's what this helps with.

You can see from the stats that the first year of growth was incredibly slow. It took around ten months for the podcast to start getting traction... and now five-plus years on, it's thriving. Can you imagine if I'd given up in the first six months because it didn't look like it was working?

Sometimes, when it feels like something is failing, it's simply building momentum. So make sure you put in enough action before deciding if something is working or not.

The only 'secret' to growth

is messy,
curious and
consistent
action.

Summary / Action

Key learnings:

1. Consistent action is key to building community.
2. A sustainable plan leads to consistent action. It's about showing up consistently, not constantly.
3. An unsustainable strategy is setting you up for failure.
4. The more imperfect you allow your action to be, the more of it you'll take.
5. Often we need to exercise self-discipline instead of waiting for motivation.
6. Taking a break, either accidentally or because you need to, is okay.
7. You've got to give something the time to succeed before you give up.

Action steps:

- Look at your strategy. Is it sustainable for you? Keep your capacity in mind.
- Reflect on how you can help yourself to be more consistent in your approach.

Abi Connick

Brand designer and mentor Abi Connick is my personal inspiration when it comes to consistency. Here's why it's been key to her success and how she keeps showing up, even when it's hard...

What does consistency mean to you?
Consistency is the backbone of my business. Without it, I'm certain it would fail. By consistently showing up and delivering content, I create a reliable reputation. This consistency is crucial in building trust with my audience. After all, who would you rather work with? Someone who consistently shows up, creates reliable content and can be counted on? Or someone who is sporadic and unpredictable, leaving you uncertain about what to expect? I know who I'd pick.

What has consistency looked like in your journey?
Consistency has been absolutely crucial to the success of my journey. This graph from my YouTube channel perfectly illustrates its significance.

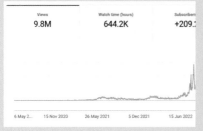

Even on those days when motivation is low, it's about having patience and resisting the urge to quit. It took a solid nine months to reach 1,000 YouTube subscribers, with each video averaging around 100 views. It would have been easy to throw in the towel, but I remained consistent, releasing videos every week, improving my camera skills, and continuously learning about YouTube. Fast forward three years and now my channel has 210K subscribers and a thriving community. This success is a testament to the power of consistency.

However, there's a crucial catch I've learned. Consistency alone won't lead to improvement if you're consistently performing poorly. It's important to combine consistency with a commitment to learning, growing and constantly striving for improvement. That's when you'll see real progress.

What has showing up consistently done for you and your business?
It has helped me build an active and engaged community. Sure, my audience size has grown, but what

'Consistency is the backbone of my business'

Growth can feel slow and frustrating at the start, but if you commit to consistency, you'll see the hard work pay off. Abi's growth on Instagram and YouTube is testament to that.

really matters is the genuine connection I have with my community. By consistently showing up and delivering valuable content, I've been able to create a loyal community that actively engages and supports my journey.

My community has come to know me as someone who shows up consistently, on good and bad days. This reliability has earned their trust, and trust is everything. This has opened up incredible opportunities for me, like creating valuable resources tailored to my community's needs, the chance to collaborate with well-known brands like Photoshop, working in person on Adobe campaigns and other exciting projects. All of these incredible opportunities stem from the trust and credibility that consistency has built with my audience.

What top three tips help you to be consistent?

1. Have a clear goal: Having a specific goal in mind provides direction and clarity. When you know what you're working towards, you can identify the consistent actions needed to achieve it.

2. Don't wait for motivation: Waiting for motivation to strike is a common mistake I see a lot of people make, which in turn is the reason for their inconsistency. Instead, understand that action creates motivation. Start taking small steps, even when you don't feel motivated. Once you get started and see progress, motivation naturally follows.

3. Define your own consistency: Consistency looks different for everyone. Set your own expectations and standards based on your capabilities and circumstances. This ensures that consistency is attainable and tailored to your journey.

Just a designer, helping designers.

Brand designer, YouTuber, educator and motivator. Just a girl sharing an insight into the branding world through fun videos!

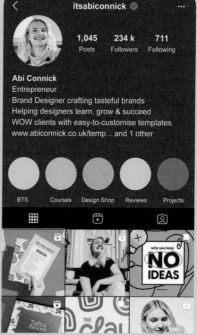

23.
How to get out of your own way

The biggest reason your strategy will succeed is you. And the biggest reason it will fail is also you.

Cheery start to the chapter, eh! But stick with me here.

As you're probably already bored of hearing, the action taken is what decides a strategy's success. So with a little logic, we can also conclude that the person taking that action is also pretty key. That is you.

(If you're not actually the person implementing the marketing, rip this chapter out and subtly slide it under the office door of whoever is.)

We can have the most clear, simple and sustainable strategy in the world, but still have something get in our way. Us.

Yep, you read that right. Despite being the ones who care most about the marketing goals and success of the strategy, we can also be the ones who stop it from happening. Put simply: we get in our own way.

The reasons behind this self-sabotage look different for all of us, but I want to touch on two of the key blocks I see people coming up against: **fear** and **lack of organization**.

In the next chapter we'll dive into the latter and how we can put systems and processes in to help ourselves, so for now let's zoom in on the big F-word: fear.

Fear

Fear is a very common feeling to come up against when you're marketing. And it makes a lot of sense.

The act of marketing, of putting yourself out there, of trying to achieve, will likely push you outside of your comfort zone. You're doing new things. Hoping for results that are uncertain. Putting your time, energy and reputation on the line. So of course fear comes up; I think that makes us human.

But does fear make us good marketers?

Fear is our brain's way of warning us not to do something that has the possibility to cause us harm. It's incredibly useful when you come up against a grizzly bear or are contemplating a skydive, but in the context of marketing I wonder if it does more harm than good.

Let's be real: the fear of a grizzly bear eyeing your family up as a light snack is slightly different to the fear of your social media not getting as many likes as you wanted it to, yet to our brain they send the same signal: get out of the way.

Whether our fear is of failing, being judged or merely not being the best, it has a sneaky way of getting us out of the 'scary' situation, thereby stopping us actioning our marketing.

Procrastination, perfectionism and a supposed lack of time are very often fear in disguise, trying to stop us from taking the action. This often subconscious behaviour may result in us feeling comfortable in the short term, but who said comfort was the route to growth?

Side-note: The fears I'm talking about here are the somewhat surface-level ones. The ones that, even if they come true, really won't have a lasting impact. If showing up via marketing brings with it a legitimate fear around lack of safety, that isn't something to trivialize and push through. Seek professional support and don't take action until you feel safe to do so.

I share this side note because when I was first being trolled in 2020, I remember feeling so deeply scared about showing up that I felt unsafe, both physically and psychologically, and kept beating myself up for not being consistent or pushing through it.

One of the biggest reasons I think we experience fear so much in marketing is because we care so much, and our identity is very often tied up in the results we get.

If I make sales, I'm a good business owner. If this post gets likes, then people like me. If my marketing is great, then I am good enough.

Any of those feel familiar? If they do, you're not alone. It's a sign you care a lot, which is great. Particularly when the business is our own or we feel particularly passionate about the mission, we can lack a separation between ourselves and the work, something that can be both helpful and detrimental.

It's easier said than done. I know seven-plus years in that I'm still on this journey, but the more we can separate our identity from our marketing, the easier things will become. If we step off the emotional rollercoaster that is tying our results to our worth, we'll be able to show up with more ease and also analyze metrics with a more objective view. It's honourable that we care so much, but it's sometimes unhealthy when we take that connection too far.

This is also true when it comes to experiencing trolling or hate comments online. That topic could be a whole book within itself, so all I'll say for now is that the more we untangle our identity and our results, the easier everything becomes.

A mindset I want to encourage you to adopt when feeling fear is to see everything in marketing as an experiment. Often our fear is that instead of getting the results we want, we'll get a negative response, such as low engagement, losing a follower, getting trolled or it not landing well.

Those situations are bound to happen in marketing, and I want you to see it as a lesson: as an opportunity to learn and grow.

The idea that 'When we take action, we either get the result we want or the lesson we need' sums this mindset up perfectly.

Instead of fearing a 'bad' result, what if we saw any outcome as a win, because we get either a result or a lesson. In my book, lessons can be far more valuable in the long run.

I'm no psychologist, so while we're not going to look at how to stop feeling fear (is that even possible?), I want to conclude this topic by looking at two main ways fear shows up and gets in the way: **perfectionism** and **comparison**.

Because I think it's less about waiting for the fear to go (spoiler alert, you'll be waiting a while!) and more about learning how to take action despite the fear, let's dive in and hear some practical tips from experts and business owners:

'My favourite quote from the Disney version of *Winnie the Pooh* is great for perfectionists to hold in mind: "You are braver than you believe, stronger than you seem, and smarter than you think."'
Natalie Englander

Resisting perfectionism

I spoke with senior cognitive behavioural therapist and mindfulness teacher Natalie Englander.

Where does perfectionism often come from?

Perfectionism isn't just about trying to be perfect; it can be a symptom of low self-worth. Therefore, perfectionism can be a way of trying to prove our worth. From a cognitive behavioural perspective, perfectionism is when our self-worth is overly dependent on striving and achievement.

Not all perfectionists realize they're perfectionists, perhaps because they feel so imperfect and think, 'I can't possibly be a perfectionist!' Or they feel pretty good on the surface, until something goes wrong, and then the low self-worth that was lying dormant gets activated.

Perfectionism can hold us back so much when marketing our businesses. Can we move past it?

Perfectionism often leads to procrastination! Break this vicious cycle by implementing practical strategies to beat procrastination.

Follow a 'good enough' mindset. I'll do a 'good enough' Instagram post or website edit. This helps to take the pressure off. And a perfectionist's version of 'good enough' is usually pretty good.

Follow the plan not the mood. Make a schedule or plan to do something (i.e. implementing a marketing strategy), and try to follow the plan, not your mood, because your mood might tell you 'nah, I can't be arsed right now, it's going to be rubbish, I need to do it when I feel I can do it perfectly'. If we follow our mood we don't know how long we'll be waiting! Motivation usually follows action.

Fake it till you make it. This can help if the pressure to do things perfectly makes you doubt yourself. Sometimes we worry this is the wrong approach, or it's not authentic, but it works. The more we do something, the more confident we feel. The less we do something, the less confident we feel. Tolerate the discomfort of things not feeling 'perfect' and do them anyway.

Exercise self-compassion. The perfect antidote to perfectionism is being kind to yourself. Motivating yourself with self-compassion is much more effective than motivating yourself with self-criticism.

Resisting comparison

Whether we're comparing ourselves to others, our past selves or where we should be, comparison can have a detrimental effect when we use it to start drawing untrue conclusions or self-judgements. I spoke with Lucy Sheridan, a comparison coach, to understand how we can navigate this.

How does comparison impact our marketing?
The way comparison impacts us is as individual as we are. However, put simply, comparison interrupts, delays and overturns the plans we make.

It can distract us on a day when we want to get lots done, sending us down a rabbit hole and taking away from the time we would've spent on our priorities. Other people's content can also lead us to question our ideas and even to conclude that we may as well not bother trying.

Comparison doesn't just slow us down, it slowly erodes our self-belief. We worry we're not clever enough, not qualified enough, not good enough. And the moment we question ourselves in this way, we cut off the oxygen to our creativity.

How can we navigate comparison?
Comparison will never go away completely, so we have to work out how to walk ourselves through it when it shows up. And it can show up quickly!

A powerful statement to talk over yourself is 'good for you and the same for me'. Use what you've seen as a reminder of how much you want that 'thing' and proof that you can achieve it. There's a physical experience that comparison can inflict too – a rising pulse, short breath and the feeling of panic. Help yourself re-centre and relax by taking slow, even, big belly breaths.

Next time comparison comes up for you, try journalling on this:

'If I'm courageous enough to be honest with myself, what's really going on here? Why am I getting so annoyed by their action? Where am I not believing in myself? And now I have that information, what work needs to happen?'

24.
Tools, automation and systems to help

As we discussed in the previous chapter, so many factors can get in the way of the implementation of our marketing strategy. Whether we like it or not, most of those factors are to do with us.

The two biggest themes I see showing up for people are <u>fear</u> and <u>poor organization</u>. We've already addressed fear, so now it's time to talk about organization.

Two truths are important to acknowledge here:

1. Time is our most limited resource.
2. We need time to take consistent action.

While it may feel like those truths contradict one another, what I take from that is that the way we use and organize our time is crucial.

Hopefully your implementation process will already get you making a clear plan of when you'll do your marketing. The next step is looking at how you can get the most out of your time, or how you can do more in less time.

Efficiency is one of my favourite things in business, because the outcome is a win/win. We either increase our output to increase results or we get more time back to rest, play or do other tasks that are important to us.

When we're looking to be more efficient, the place we need to go to is in our habits, systems and processes; that is, the things we put into place behind the scenes that don't feel super exciting, but will help us to do more in less time.

'You don't rise to your goals, you fall to your systems' is one of my favourite quotes by James Clear (*Atomic Habits*), as it reminds us of the role that systems play.

It's easy to feel excited about our goals and assume that will be enough. However, as we likely know all too well, motivation is fickle and before long our goals alone won't be enough to keep us taking action.

Three ways to increase efficiency

When looking for ways to save time in your marketing, there are three possible solutions on hand. Before we look at those, it's important we know which tasks we're looking to optimize. Here's an exercise that will set you up well:

1. **List out all of the tasks you do within your marketing.** Everything from planning and creating to replying to comments and analyzing metrics. Write a list of every single job and, if it helps you to see them clearly, organize them by theme.
2. **Assign each task a value from 1 to 3.** Tasks have varying levels of importance, so spend time considering if the task is 1) high impact, 2) needs to be done or 3) low impact. 'Impact' should be defined by how pivotal a role that task plays in achieving your goals.
3. **Reflect on the amount of time each task takes.** Assign each task as A, B or C. A = takes up too much time; B = takes up a fair amount of time; C = not enough time is spent on this. You may need to spend a few days tracking your time to understand what each task requires.

You should then be left with a complete view of your marketing tasks, their importance and their time.

The purpose of this exercise is to help you identify which tasks are most in need of optimizing. We can't improve everything at once, so here's my recommendation:

TIP
If you feel overwhelmed doing every task at once, take it one topic or platform at a time. For example, just look at the social media tasks, or only the content creation tasks.

	High impact 1	Needs to be done 2	Low impact 3
Takes too much time A	⬤	⬜	⬤
Takes fair amount of time B	⬤	⬤	⬜
Not enough time C	⬤	⬤	⬤

⬤ Action first   ⬜ Next   ⬤ Leave until last

Starting with your high-priority tasks, consider how you can do one of the three things below to increase your efficiency:

Streamline

Introduce a way of completing the task that makes it easier to complete.

- Create templates for your graphic design.
- Collate a folder of images and videos to choose from when creating content.
- Upload your fonts, brand colours and logos to your design software.
- Add a form to your website that makes it easier for potential clients to make enquiries.
- Utilize artificial intelligence to complete research or analysis on your behalf.
- Create a dedicated email address for press and media outreach and enquiries.
- Use transcription tools to turn video or audio content into a written format.
- Automate your social media DM replies.
- Store all your passwords in one place for easy access.

Reminder: these actions may feel like they're using up your precious time to set up, but once they're complete, they will save you time in the long term. Short-term work for long-term benefit, that's what streamlining is about!

Delegate

Outsource the task, or an element of it, to someone else.

- Involve one of your current team members more within your marketing.
- Find a freelancer or a virtual assistant who can fulfil these tasks.
- Build a network of freelancers who can support you with one-off projects and tasks.
- Outsource your content creation to a social media manager.
- Hire a designer to create graphic templates for you to use.
- Centralize your brand guidelines, strategies and assets to make it easier for others to work with you.
- Work with a community manager to stay on top of messages and comments.

Eliminate

Get rid of a task, because it doesn't serve a purpose.

So often we do tasks because they used to be valuable or because other businesses we know do them, but that doesn't mean they are right for us. If you're looking for permission to take something off your plate that doesn't need to be there, here it is.

PERMISSION SLIP
I am giving myself permission to stop:

And therefore giving myself more time and energy to focus on the actions which are most importat to me.

TIP
When you're working with a team, be okay with the fact that they will probably never care about your business as much as you do. That's to be expected.

How it's done

Katie Chappell, live event illustration specialist, used to find herself trying things that weren't for her.

'It's easy to feel like we're the problem and just push through, but why don't we start looking at changing the plan to work for you?'

I asked Katie what practical steps she's taken to make her marketing work for her, and it's given me some great ideas:

- Invest in assets that help customers understand how I can help them, such as a professional video explaining how I work.
- Create email templates! Don't reinvent the wheel every time you write to a client.
- Look at data and see what's pulling its weight. Which blog posts are keeping people on your site? What's getting people to request a quote? Who's saying nice things about you to their colleagues? Find what's working and do more of that.
- Schedule posts in advance. Some days I have loads of ideas and energy for writing so I make the most of those times and I have a spreadsheet with all of my ideas ready to go.
- Outsource the bits I'm really bad at. I have help with email inbox management, replying to enquiries and following up with enquiries.

You never reach peak efficiency

This exercise, of mapping out your tasks and picking a way to make them more efficient, is something you'll have to do many times in your business. As our priorities change, our goals shift and our businesses evolve, and our approach to time management will need to change too.

This is a good exercise to do once a year in your business, and at any points in between where you're lacking efficiency but can't see why that is or how to fix it.

TIP
This isn't about becoming robots and being as efficient as possible. It's about taking the messy action that will lead to real progress.

Summary / Action

Key learnings:

1. Increasing efficiency allows us to either increase our output or spend more time doing the other tasks that matter to us.
2. Before looking to change our systems and processes, we first need to understand which tasks are the priority.
3. There are three core ways to improve a task: streamline, delegate and eliminate.
4. Improving our systems and processes isn't a one-time thing; it's something we need to revisit as our business evolves.

Action steps:

- Complete the exercise to understand which tasks are high priority for you to improve.
- Take the action to streamline, delegate or eliminate some of your priority tasks. Remember: just doing one thing will pay dividends in the long run!

25.
How to stay curious and track success

Take messy, *curious* and consistent action.

We round off this conversation by looking at the curiosity element of that commitment.

It's all one big experiment

In marketing, it can be easy to get caught up in the results and get too attached to the outcome. This mindset means that when things are going well we feel on top of the world (yay!), but also means that when the opposite is true and we don't see the results we want, we feel awful.

I call this the rollercoaster of results. It is somewhat exhilarating but a pretty exhausting way to feel when we're taking action.

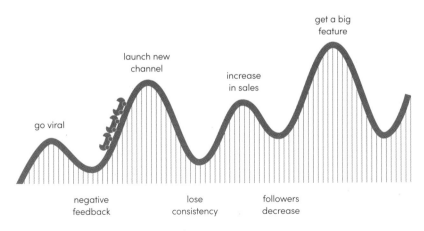

get a big
feature

launch new
channel

increase
in sales

go viral

negative
feedback

lose
consistency

followers
decrease

In fact, it isn't just an unenjoyable way of showing up, it also means we're approaching our results in the wrong way. Simply deciding that a 'bad' result is bad and leaving it at that means that we're missing out on the valuable lessons that may sit within that experience.

The better way to look at it is that when we take action, we get a mixture of wins and lessons. And both of those results hold valuable information.

- The wins show us what's working and what to do more of.
- The lessons tell us what isn't working and how we may need to or want to improve.

When we look at our results in this way, we start seeing our marketing as an experiment, which is a far more enjoyable and helpful way of looking at things. When it's all one big experiment, we shouldn't be scared of getting a 'bad' result, we should see it as progress.

From where I'm standing, it's far better to take a piece of action that doesn't work out and leave with a lesson than to do nothing and stay where you are.

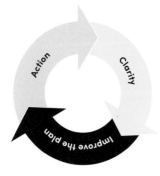

Metrics

One of the best ways to stay curious and benefit from the lessons that your action will be teaching you is to look at your metrics.

Alice Benham Dictionary
Metrics: the data you choose to track, which measures and indicates the performance of your marketing strategy.

Let's break down the two types of metrics we can track:

Measures

These metrics directly rate to your end goal and tell you that your marketing strategy is working. For example, if your goal is organic sales, a measure metric would be your website revenue attributed to social media. Or if your goal is visibility, your measure metric may be your audience size or traffic.

Indicators

These metrics are a sign that your marketing goals are on track to being achieved. They're great to track so that you can see the progress you're making before your 'measure metrics' start to kick in.

It's important to define the difference between the two, because it's easy to start seeing our indicator metrics as our measures of success. We get caught up in our follow number, likes on a post or email unsubscribes, when in reality these are nothing more than vanity metrics or, at best, indicators of our success.

Also, not every metric matters! Whether it's on your social media, website or podcast, every platform will bombard you with a hoard of facts and figures, but just because a metric is available to you doesn't mean it needs to be tracked.

Choosing which metrics to track

If you try to track every metric available to you, you'll quickly feel overwhelmed and stop looking at any metrics. The metrics you choose to track will determine how valuable you find it, so choose wisely.

The key thing to consider is: which metric will best measure or indicate that I am achieving my marketing goals?

Check in with yourself: <u>what are you trying to achieve on this platform?</u>

Then consider: <u>which of these metrics relate to that?</u>

Make sure your metrics either measure or indicate that you're on track for your goals.

If you're stuck on where to begin, here are a few universal metrics I think we can all find value in tracking:

- Social media: engagement percentage, click-throughs to other platforms.
- Email marketing: open rate, click-through rate.
- Website: traffic sources, session duration, bounce rate.
- Sales: total revenue, average order value, conversion rate, repeat purchase rate.

You'll notice none of these are vanity metrics showing us follower count or total subscribers; they're behavioural metrics that indicate the behaviour and engagement *within* our community. What good is a big crowd if none of them are listening?

How to track

Making time each month to step back, track your metrics and learn from them is a habit I'd suggest every business builds.

Here are my top tips for getting the most out of this time:

- **Put the time in your schedule.** This task likely won't feel fun or exciting, so exercise self-discipline and make it happen.
- **Consider any qualitative reflections that feel relevant.** Was it a month where you took some time off from social media? Do you feel like you nailed your marketing processes this month? These are all valuable to acknowledge too.
- **Take time to investigate your metrics once they're collated.** If you notice something that seems off, such as a noticeable dip or rise in a particular metric, reflect on why this could be.
- **Look for the lessons.** Tracking metrics isn't about making cool spreadsheets; it's about learning. Note down three to five key lessons or reminders that you can draw from the data you've gathered.

- **Make small but intentional changes to your strategy.** Try not to give yourself strategy whiplash by changing the whole plan every month. Instead, look to make a couple of small but intentional changes and, most importantly, commit to those changes before trying something new.
- **Let any new strategy settle before you track too intensely.** If you've made a big change or are doing something new, give the metrics a bit of time to find their 'normal' before you interrogate them. Remember what we chatted about in Chapter 20? We need to put in consistent action before we start judging the results too closely.

Celebrating wins

I could easily end this chapter here now we've discussed the serious-and-important-metric-tracking stuff, but that would mean missing out on something that is also important: celebrating our wins!

In our desire to be constantly improving, we can be so focused on what didn't go right or needs to change that we fail to acknowledge and celebrate our success, which I think is a real shame.

Now before you roll your eyes at me for suggesting such a 'silly' topic in a marketing book, let me make a case for why celebration is key to your marketing success.

Self-celebration builds belief.

Studies show that positive self-talk can increase cognitive performance,* so if you show your brain evidence that you are great at X, you'll take more confident and consistent action in that.

On top of that very scientific case for self-celebration, how about doing it because it feels good? Working for and by yourself is hard enough, without you being hard on yourself unnecessarily, so be a great boss to yourself and celebrate the good stuff. Because nobody else will do it for you!

Here are my top tips for celebrating your wins:

- **List them out, *all* of them.** It's easy to let the wins pass you by, so build a regular habit of writing them somewhere. I have a document on my desktop that I open at the end of every week and add my wins to, big and small. Sometimes I'm celebrating hitting a huge goal and sometimes I'm just proud of myself for showing up.
- **Create a happy folder.** Every time you receive a kind email, nice comment or hit a metric milestone, screenshot it and put it in a happy folder. This folder can be there when you need a reminder of why you do what you do.
- **Find ways of self-celebration that are meaningful to you.** We all have different ways of feeling celebrated and loved, so find yours! Is it writing it down? Sharing it with someone else? Buying yourself a treat to acknowledge it?
- **Share your wins with people who get it.** You *may* find that family and friends who aren't into marketing don't *quite* understand the thing you're celebrating, so sometimes sharing the win with someone who 'gets it' (a business friend or your network) will feel better.

> **TIP**
> Gather your metrics in a tool that you find easy to fill out and read. I personally love a spreadsheet. They're not particularly fancy, but they do the job and can do calculations on your behalf!

*Source: www.ncbi.nlm.nih.gov/pmc/articles/PMC8295361/

Summary / Action

Key learnings:

1. Clarity comes from action, so make time to step back and learn.
2. Metrics are a valuable way of learning from our action, so we can improve our marketing strategy moving forwards.
3. There are two types of metrics to track: indicators and measures.
4. Viewing marketing as an experiment will help us to find valuable lessons in our challenges, as opposed to seeing them as a bad thing.
5. Celebrating wins will do more than just make you feel good; it will help you take more confident and consistent action in future.

Action steps:

- Decide which metrics are relevant for you to track.
- Put a time in your schedule each month to check in on your metrics and learn from them.
- Pick a place to list out your wins, big and small.
- Create a happy folder on your phone or laptop to put positive evidence in.

Clarity comes from action,

so make time
to step back
and learn.

Conclusion

If you're reading this chapter that tells me you've either skipped to the end to figure out how the book ends, or you've finished reading.

If you're in the first camp, I hate to break it to you but this isn't that kind of book... but please do head to Chapter 1 and we'll see you back here soon!

But if you've made it through the whole book, well done, you brilliant human.

Making the time to work 'on' your business is no small feat. I'm aware that marketing can be an overwhelming topic for many, so I am so proud of you for making it through.

I know I've shared a lot within this book (I'm not sure I have anything left to say about marketing at this point...), but I want you to take away what has felt relevant for you. Trust yourself to carry with you any action that is going to help you, and feel free to forget the rest. You can always come back and read that section again when you're ready!

Remember: your marketing strategy should evolve over time, so action what you've created (even if you don't feel ready!) and make time in the future to revisit and refine it. Any change in your business, shift in consumer behaviour and marketing evolutions should nudge you to tweak your marketing strategy.

As we conclude this journey together, I am sending a whole lot of encouragement your way as you keep taking action. Let it be imperfect. Look for the lessons. Be kind to yourself. And remember: you've got this.

I'll be cheering you on.

AB
x

Index

Acknowledgements

The first and biggest thank you goes to Liz Faber at Laurence King for approaching me to write this book – your faith in me, encouragement and patience throughout has been invaluable. And, a huge thank you to the rest of the team for their expert input: Catherine Hooper, Charlie Bolton and Nicola Hodgson.

To my clients, students and community, you've played a key role in sharpening my expertise and supporting my journey. Thank you to every contributor in this book who has generously shared their story and knowledge, and also to Molly and Fi for providing guidance when I first got my book deal. Huge thanks to my friends and family for being my biggest cheerleaders from day one. And thank you to RSM for moving out of the flat for four days to let me speed write this book in peace. You're all heroes.

Picture credits

All graphics by Charlie Bolton
p. 6: Author portrait taken in Candid Studios, www.candidstudios.co.uk
pp. 26 and 27: photos – Donna Ford @donnafordography (insta) and www.donnaford.co.uk.
pp. 76 and 77: Screenshots – Sasha Gupta
p. 87: Photos – Emily Marcovecchio, www.emilyanna.net; screenshots – Alice Benham; Podcast artwork – Bron Findlay, From Finn, www.fromfinn.com
p. 101, bottom row: photos – Amy Grover, www.amygroverphoto.co.uk
pp. 112 and 113: Forbes articles – Bianca Barratt
p. 113, right: headshot – Luke Sampson
p. 131: photo – Nadine Sabrina, Nadine Sabrina Photography, www.nadinesabrina-photography.com
p. 132: screenshots – Sophie Miller, Pretty Little Marketer
p. 143: Rachel Harris
p. 145, bottom: photo – Hermione Hodgson, www.hermionehodgson.com
p. 150: photo – Rachel Waring, www.rachelemmawaring.com